QUEUE

ACT/SAT Math Word Problems

by Jonathan D. Kantrowitz

Item Code QWK9601 • Copyright © 2017 Queue, Inc.

Queue, Inc • P.O. Box 156, Fairfield, CT 06824

(800) 232-2224 • Fax: (800) 775-2729 • www.qworkbooks.com

Teacher Edition available: jdk@queueinc.com

Table of Contents

Formula Sheet

Length

Metric

1 kilometer = 1,000 meters
1 meter = 100 centimeters
1 centimeter = 10 millimeters

Customary

1 foot = 12 inches
1 yard = 3 feet = 36 inches
1 mile = 5,280 feet = 1,760 yards

Capacity and Volume

Metric

1 liter (L) = 1,000 milliliters (mL)
1,000 cubic centimeters = 1,000 mL

Customary

1 cup = 8 ounces
1 pint = 2 cups = 16 ounces
1 quart = 2 pints = 32 ounces
1 gallon = 4 quarts = 128 ounces

Time

1 minute = 60 seconds
1 hour = 60 minutes = 3,600 seconds
1 day = 24 hours = 1,440 minutes
1 week = 7 days = 168 hours
1 year = 52 weeks = 12 months
1 year = 365 days

Mass and Weight

Metric

1 kilogram = 1,000 grams
1 gram = 1,000 milligrams

Customary

1 pound = 16 ounces
1 ton = 2,000 pounds

Metric and Customary Equivalents

Linear Measure

1 inch = 2.54 centimeters
1 foot = .3048 meters
1 mile = 1.6093 kilometers
1 meter = 3.2808 feet
1 kilometer = .62137 miles

Liquid Measure

1 fluid ounce = 29.573 milliliters
1 liter = 1.0567 quarts
1 gallon = 3.7854 liters

Weights

1 ounce = 28.350 grams
1 pound = .45359 kilograms
1 kilogram = 2.2046 pounds

Formula Sheet

Square

perimeter = $4s$
area = s^2

Rectangle

perimeter = $2w + 2l$
area = $l \bullet w$

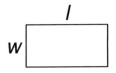

Triangle

area = $1/2(b \bullet h)$

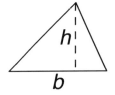

Trapezoid

area = $1/2(b_1 + b_2)h$

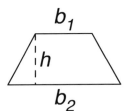

Parallelogram

area = $b \bullet h$

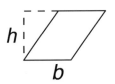

Circle

Circumference = $2\pi r$
Area = πr^2

Pythagorean Theorem

$a^2 + b^2 = c^2$

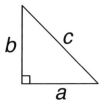

Rectangular Solid

volume = $l \bullet w \bullet h$
surface area =
$2lw + 2lh + 2wh$

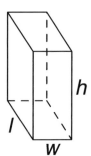

Cylinder

volume = $\pi r^2 h$
lateral surface area
= $2\pi rh$
surface area =
$2\pi r^2 + 2\pi rh$

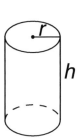

Sphere

surface area = $4\pi r^2$
volume = $4/3(\pi r^3)$

Cone

lateral surface area
= πrs
surface area =
$\pi rs + \pi r^2$
volume = $1/3(\pi r^2 h)$

2

Item	Servings Sold
Regular Cones	140
Waffles Cones	119
Cups	65
Sundaes	40
Milkshakes	86

1. The owner of a homemade ice cream shop constructs a circle graph to compare the amounts of various items sold. He uses sales during the month of July, shown in the above table, to create the graph. What central angle should be used for the section of the circle representing sundaes?

    a. 11.25°
    b. 16°
    c. 32°
    d. 40°

2. Lori needs to purchase 482 feet of fabric to make curtains. The fabric costs $0.43 per yard. Which of the following amounts is CLOSEST to the amount of money Lori needs to purchase the fabric?

    a. $11.00
    b. $17.00
    c. $70.00
    d. $160.00

3. Lenny tried to calculate $\sqrt[3]{60}$ on his calculator and got an answer of 7.75. He wondered if this answer was reasonable. Which of the following explains the reasonableness of his answer?

    a. It is reasonable because $7.75^2 = 60$.
    b. It is not reasonable because the answer should be an integer.
    c. It is not reasonable because $3^3 = 27$ and $4^3 = 64$, so the answer should be between 3 and 4.
    d. It is reasonable because the answer should be slightly less than 8.

4. Estimate $\sqrt{130}$ to determine which of the following statements is TRUE.

    a. $\sqrt{130} > 12$
    b. $\sqrt{130} < 11$
    c. $\sqrt{130} = 11$
    d. $\sqrt{130} > 11$

5. You and your friends paid $10.45 for a pizza. If you ate 2 of the 8 pieces of the pizza, about how much should you pay for your share?

    a. $1.31
    b. $2.09
    c. $2.61
    d. $5.23

8. It takes two pounds of basil leaves to make one and a half ounces of pesto. How many pounds of basil are needed to make 13 ounces of pesto?

    a. 8 2/3 pounds
    b. 17 1/3 pounds
    c. 26 pounds
    d. 52 pounds

6. A square has an area of 202 square inches. Which of the following measures is CLOSEST to the length of one of its sides?

    a. 13.6 inches
    b. 14.2 inches
    c. 14.8 inches
    d. 50.5 inches

9. A cube has a volume of 117 cubic inches. Which of the following measures is CLOSEST to the length of one of its sides?

    a. 4.9
    b. 4
    c. 4.2
    d. 5

7. If -9 is multiplied by a number less than -1, which of the following BEST describes the result?

    a. a number less than -9
    b. a number greater than -9
    c. a number between -9 and 9
    d. a number greater than 9

10. Estimate $\sqrt{70}$ to determine which of the following statements is TRUE.

    a. $\sqrt{70} > 9$

    b. $\sqrt{70} > 8$

    c. $\sqrt{70} = 9$

    d. $\sqrt{70} < 8$

11. Meredith is 5 feet, 6 inches tall and casts a 3-foot-long shadow. At the same time, a tree casts a 10.5-foot shadow. Which of the following proportions can be used to find the height of the tree?

   a. $h/10.5 = 5.6/3$
   b. $3/h = 5.5/10.6$
   c. $3/10.5 = 5.6/h$
   d. $5.5/3 = h/10.5$

12. Approximately one third of the town's 2,167 residents attended the annual block party. Which of the following is CLOSEST to the number of people who did not attend?

   a. 650
   b. 720
   c. 1,300
   d. 1,440

13. About one-eighth of the population is left-handed. If there are 48 left-handed students at the high school, how many students can you expect attend the school?

   a. 324
   b. 384
   c. 600
   d. 640

14. The population of Canton increased from 10,000 citizens in 1995 to 12,000 citizens in 2000. By what percent did the population increase?

   a. 2%
   b. 17%
   c. 20%
   d. 117%

15. During a group's fundraiser, $2.00 per item sold goes to a charity. F, the total amount raised, is represented by the equation $F = 2n + 55$, where n is the number of items sold. If the group sold between 550 and 700 items, then the total amount of money raised should be between which of the following?

    a. $1,055.00 and $1,555.00
    b. $1,045.00 and $1,345.00
    c. $1,155.00 and $1,455.00
    d. $1,100.00 and $1,400.00

16. The distance from Atlanta, Georgia to Dallas, Texas is approximately 1,256 kilometers. If 1 mile = 1.609 kilometers, what is the approximate distance, in miles, between Atlanta and Dallas?

    a. 750 miles
    b. 780 miles
    c. 1,240 miles
    d. 2,020 miles

17. Jahna is keeping a database of customer information. If it takes her 35 minutes to enter 10% of the customer information into the database, how many hours will it take to enter all of the data?

    a. 5 5/6 hours
    b. 3 1/2 hours
    c. 350 hours
    d. 28 4/7 hours

18. Approximately one quarter of the town's 1,127 residents voted in the last election. Which of the following is CLOSEST to the number of people who did not vote?

    a. 370
    b. 280
    c. 560
    d. 850

Depth of a River

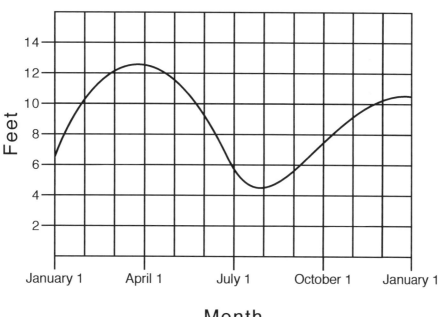

Month

The above graph gives the average depth of a local river.

19. Which of the following would be the approximate difference between the highest and lowest water levels?

   a. 5 feet
   b. 8 feet
   c. 11 feet
   d. 14 feet

20. Which of the following would be a REASONABLE ESTIMATE of the average depth of the river?

   a. 8.50 feet
   b. 10.25 feet
   c. 6.00 feet
   d. 9.75 feet

Math and Science Degrees Awarded

Year	Number of Degrees Awarded
1960	24
1970	47
1980	95
1990	191
2000	384

21. A local college has been tracking the number of Math and Science degrees it has awarded to women over the past 40 years. This information is shown in the above table. Which of the following would be a REASONABLE ESTIMATE of the number of Math and Science degrees to be awarded to women in the year 2010?

    a. 450
    b. 520
    c. 580
    d. 770

22. At a local electronics store, all DVDs are 15% off. Paula buys five DVDs that originally cost $15.99 each. How much money does she save as a result of the sale?

    a. $15.00
    b. $15.99
    c. $11.99
    d. $64.95

23. Valerie's French class contains 24 students. If the ratio of girls to boys is 5 to 3, how many boys are in the class?

    a. 8
    b. 9
    c. 7
    d. 10

8

24. Claire has a paper that she expects will take her 24 hours to write for her Modern American Novel Class. She completes 3/8 of the paper by the end of Tuesday and then works three hours each day on Wednesday and Thursday. She works for four hours on Friday and does not work on Saturday. She must finish the paper on Sunday since it is due Monday. How many hours will Claire have to spend working on the paper on Sunday?

    a. 3 hours
    b. 4 hours
    c. 5 hours
    d. 10 hours

25. On a map the distance from Boston, MA to Hartford, CT is 13.5 inches. If the map's scale claims that one inch is approximately 7 miles, what is the distance from Boston to Hartford?

    a. 94.5 miles
    b. 96.0 miles
    c. 103.5 miles
    d. 186.0 miles

26. To qualify for the New York City Marathon which is 26.2 miles in length, Frank must complete another marathon in 3 hours and 15 minutes. How fast must Frank run, in miles per hour, in order to complete 26.2 miles in 3 hours and 15 minutes, rounded to the nearest tenth.

    a. 8.1 miles per hour
    b. 9.4 miles per hour
    c. 6.7 miles per hour
    d. 7.2 miles per hour

27. In Mrs. Cheng's math class, the ratio of boys to girls is 7 to 5. If there are 24 students in her class, how many are girls?

    a. 16
    b. 14
    c. 12
    d. 10

A space shuttle is 2.99×10^7 meters from Earth traveling toward Earth at 4.5 km/min.

28. ABOUT how long will it take the space shuttle to reach Earth?

    a. 4 days, 14 hours, and 45 minutes
    b. 5 days, 4 hours, and 45 minutes
    c. 12 days, 6 hours, and 30 minutes
    d. 108 days, 12 hours, and 15 minutes

29. ABOUT how fast, in km/hour, would the shuttle have to travel to reach Earth in three days?

    a. 208 km/hr
    b. 315 km/hr
    c. 345 km/hr
    d. 415 km/hr

30. The speed of light is approximately 3.0×10^8 meters per second. How many times faster does light travel compared to the shuttle?

    a. 2 times faster
    b. 4,000,000 times faster
    c. 8,000 times faster
    d. 64,000 times faster

Hawaii Flag

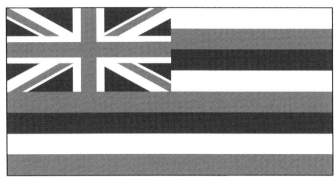

Color Key
Red   Blue   White

31. Hawaii, in 1959, became the last state to enter the United States. The picture shown above is a scaled drawing of the Hawaiian state flag. Which of the following would be a REASONABLE ESTIMATE of what fraction of the flag is red?

    a. 7/16
    b. 1/4
    c. 3/8
    d. 3/16

32. The Stallions won 60% of their games this year. They had 16 losses and 2 ties. Which of the following would be the ratio of wins to losses?

    a. 25 to 18
    b. 27 to 16
    c. 14 to 9
    d. 27 to 43

33. The ratio of the angles in a triangle is 3 to 4 to 5. What would be the measure of the smallest angle?

    a. 15°
    b. 33°
    c. 45°
    d. 54°

34. Cory's family gave him $150.00 for his birthday. He goes to the Mall of America and spends 1/4 of his money on CDs and 2/5 of his money on sneakers. How much money does he have left when he finishes shopping?

   a. $97.50
   b. $67.50
   c. $52.50
   d. $45.00

36. A company produces 1,200 light bulbs per day and is open five days per week. In a random sample of 25 light bulbs, three were defective. How many light bulbs manufactured in the factory are defective each week?

   a. 96 bulbs
   b. 360 bulbs
   c. 450 bulbs
   d. 720 bulbs

35. An eight-foot statue casts a 3 1/3-foot shadow. How tall, in inches, is a statue that casts a five-foot shadow?

   a. 12 inches
   b. 54 inches
   c. 96 inches
   d. 144 inches

37. If a grocer buys 18 bagels for $3.96, how much does she pay for an order of 96 bagels?

   a. $287.82
   b. $21.12
   c. $14.63
   d. $8.96

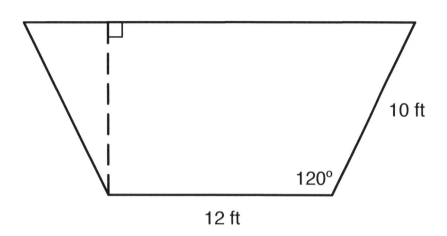

38. A builder is constructing eight homes in a cul-de-sac. He wants to build a deck on each home in the shape of an isosceles trapezoid. The deck's dimensions are shown above. Which of the following would be the area of one deck?

    a. 147.22 square feet
    b. 172.84 square feet
    c. 178.06 square feet
    d. 136.19 square feet

39. In the first ten games of the season, Sue made 35 out of 41 foul shots. If she shoots a total of 700 fouls shots for the season, how many of the remaining 659 foul shots would she have to make to make 88% of her shots for the season?

    a. 561
    b. 564
    c. 569
    d. 581

40. John buys a hat for $17.50, a pair of sneakers for $97.99, and a pair of sweat pants for $21.49. If every item in the store is 10% off, what will be his total bill including 5% sales tax?

    a. $129.45
    b. $150.13
    c. $166.39
    d. $205.47

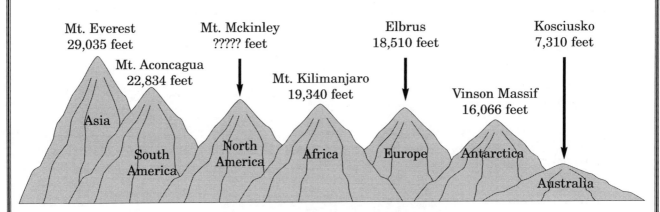

| Mt. Everest 29,035 feet | Mt. Mckinley ????? feet | Elbrus 18,510 feet | Kosciusko 7,310 feet |

Mt. Aconcagua 22,834 feet

Mt. Kilimanjaro 19,340 feet

Vinson Massif 16,066 feet

Asia

South America

North America

Africa

Europe

Antarctica

Australia

The Seven Summits

About 95 mountaineers have climbed to the highest points on each continent, known as the "Seven Summits." The above diagram shows the highest points of each of these seven mountains.

41. Based on the information in the diagram, which of the following could be the height of Mt. McKinley?

    a. 17,176 feet
    b. 19,425 feet
    c. 21,024 feet
    d. 22,921 feet

42. If a climber has scaled all seven mountains, approximately how many miles has he or she climbed in doing so?

43. Carlos runs three miles per day, five days a week. He is planning to run a half-marathon which is 13.1 miles in length. At a running clinic, a coach told Carlos that he should be running 24 miles per week for at least five weeks prior to the half-marathon and that he should not increase his mileage by more than 5% each week. If Carlos follows his coach's advice, when can he enter his first half-marathon?

    a. in 5 weeks
    b. in 10 weeks
    c. in 15 weeks
    d. in 18 weeks

44. Sarah went for a four-hour run. For the first two hours, her average speed was 5.5 miles per hour. For the last hour, her average speed was 4.25 miles per hour. What was her average speed for the third hour if her average speed for the entire run was five miles per hour?

    a. 5.75 mph
    b. 5.25 mph
    c. 5.00 mph
    d. 4.75 mph

45. Carolyn builds a scale model of an antique car. Her model is 14 inches long and 8 inches wide. If the actual car is 9.5 feet long, about how wide is the actual car, rounded to the nearest tenth of a foot?

    a. 5.4 feet wide
    b. 5.8 feet wide
    c. 6.0 feet wide
    d. 7.2 feet wide

15

Tyler's Painting Company has been hired to paint an entire 15-room house. Tyler, the owner of the company, has five employees and each employee makes $120.00 per day for eight hours of work. Tyler works with the crew but does not draw a weekly salary. With six people (himself and the crew) working, he expects the job to take four days.

46. How much will Tyler pay out for employee salaries for this job?

    a. $3,200.00
    b. $2,800.00
    c. $2,400.00
    d. $2,100.00

47. Tyler remembers that two of his employees are going on vacation so he considers hiring two replacements for this job, at a salary of $90.00 per day. How much money would he save on the entire job by paying the two replacements instead of the two employees from his regular crew?

    a. $240.00
    b. $210.00
    c. $180.00
    d. $60.00

48. Tyler is unable to find replacements so the job must now be done by four people. How many days will the job take with four people working instead of six?

    a. 4 days
    b. 5.5 days
    c. 6 days
    d. 7 days

49. Using the information in the above problem, the owner of the house insists that the job gets done in four days. How many total extra hours would each employee, including Tyler, have to work to get the job done in four days?

    a. 10 hours
    b. 12 hours
    c. 14 hours
    d. 16 hours

Average Cost of Homes

Year	Average Cost
2000	$299,000
2001	$313,000
2002	$330,000
2003	$347,000
2004	$365,000

50. The average cost of homes in a community has been increasing in each of the past five years according to the above chart. Using the information in the above chart, which of the following would be the MOST REASONABLE prediction of the average cost of a home in this community in the year 2008?

    a. $475,000
    b. $367,000
    c. $444,000
    d. $395,000

51. A plumber charges $89.00 to come to your house plus $75.00 per hour for the actual work done. If a plumber is at your house for 2 hours and 20 minutes, what is the total bill?

    a. $264.00
    b. $175.00
    c. $283.00
    d. $239.00

52. On a map, 1/4 inch represents 30 miles. How far apart, in miles, are two towns that are 3 1/2 inches apart on the map?

    a. 540 miles
    b. 360 miles
    c. 240 miles
    d. 420 miles

53. Sarah learned that scientists have discovered an asteroid traveling toward Earth at 87,000 km per minute. The asteroid is currently 5.24×10^8 km from Earth. NASA scientists must come up with a plan to destroy the asteroid before it comes within 3.27×10^4 km of Earth or debris from the asteroid will land on this planet. ABOUT How many days do the NASA scientists have?

    a. 4.2 days
    b. 15.6 days
    c. 16.4 days
    d. 90.3 days

54. Fred, Nelson, and Omar decide to go into business together. Omar invests $70,000.00, Nelson invests $50,000.00, and Fred invests $20,000.00. They agree to split the profits in the same ratio as the amounts invested. If the profit for their first year was $112,000.00, how much did Nelson receive?

    a. $8,000.00
    b. $40,000.00
    c. $50,000.00
    d. $56,000.00

55. Al's Hamburger Shop held a hamburger eating contest last month. Sonny won the contest by eating 24 hamburgers in eight minutes. At that rate, how many hamburgers had Sonny eaten in six minutes?

    a. 10
    b. 12
    c. 15
    d. 18

Numerical Reasoning

The table below shows the number of runs the Sharks, a local softball team, scored over a ten-game span. Use this information to answer the following questions.

Game	1	2	3	4	5	6	7	8	9	10
Sharks	6	3	7	5	8	0	3	3	2	6
Opponents	4	1	8	4	3	1	1	0	1	7

56. What percent of their games did the Sharks win?

    a. 54%
    b. 67%
    c. 70%
    d. 75%

57. If the Sharks lose four out of their next five games, what percent of their total games have they won then?

    a. 50.25%
    b. 53.33%
    c. 57.68%
    d. 64.13%

58. If the team plays sixty games in a full season, and they continue to win at the rate shown in the table, how many total games will they win?

    a. 27 games
    b. 28 games
    c. 31 games
    d. 42 games

59. Over the ten games shown in the above table, one player scored 15 of the Sharks' runs. ABOUT what percent of the team's total runs did this player score?

    a. 35%
    b. 45%
    c. 50%
    d. 33%

60. Sonia is training to run a half-marathon which is 13 miles in length. Sonia's training schedule in to run two miles every Monday, Wednesday, and Friday and six miles every Tuesday and Thursday. She also runs eight miles every Saturday. At the end of ten weeks of her training schedule, Sonia would have run the equivalent of how many half-marathons?

    a. 10
    b. 12
    c. 20
    d. 32

61. The measures of the angles of a triangle are in the ratio of 1 to 2 to 3. What would be the measure of the SMALLEST angle?

    a. 30°
    b. 15°
    c. 45°
    d. 60°

62. Meghan makes $37.50 per hour for the first 40 hours she works each week as a pharmacist. For any hours over 40, she earns 1.5 times her standard hourly salary. Last week she worked 46.5 hours. How much money did she earn?

    a. $1,865.63
    b. $2,250.00
    c. $1,743.75
    d. $1,837.75

63. Karisa solves 2.5 math problems in 15 minutes. At the same rate, how many math problems will she solve in one hour?

    a. 5
    b. 10
    c. 12
    d. 15

On Wednesdays, Nancy's Pizza Parlor in New Haven gives every 15th customer a free slice of pizza and every 25th customer a free order of bread sticks. Last Wednesday there were 360 customers.

64. How many orders of bread sticks did they give away last Wednesday?

    a. 12
    b. 14
    c. 15
    d. 32

65. If a large pizza contains eight slices, how many pizzas did they give away last Wednesday?

    a. 2
    b. 3
    c. 4
    d. 24

66. When Shaun went to Nancy's Pizza, the cashier told him that he was the first person to get both a free slice of pizza and a free order of bread sticks. How many customers were ahead of Shaun?

    a. 25
    b. 74
    c. 37
    d. 149

67. How many customers received something for free at Nancy's last Wednesday?

    a. 25
    b. 34
    c. 38
    d. 45

68. Nancy's Pizza Parlor is open from 3:00 p.m. to 10:00 p.m. What is the average number of customers per hour, rounded to the nearest whole number?

    a. 43
    b. 45
    c. 51
    d. 58

Day	1	2	3	4	5
End of Day Total	6	14	22	30	38

69. The above table shows that a furniture factory produced a total of 38 rocking chairs during the first five days of production. On which day will the company produce its 300th rocking chair?

   a. the 27th day
   b. the 38th day
   c. the 39th day
   d. the 41st day

70. John found 36 shells during a walk on the beach. Each shell was either a conch or a clamshell. If the ratio of conch to clam shells was 3 to 1, how many conch shells did John find?

   a. 9
   b. 12
   c. 18
   d. 27

71. At the end of summer sale, a lawn mower is on sale for 25% off of the original price. If the sale price is $532.49, find the original cost of the lawn mower.

   a. $177.50
   b. $399.37
   c. $665.61
   d. $709.99

In March, Polar Bear Air Conditioning Company conducted a survey of families in 200 homes . The families were chosen as a representative sample from a list of 3,000 families identified as potential customers for Arctic Blast, Polar Bear's new, state-of-the-art, energy-efficient central air conditioning unit. The results of the survey are shown below.

Question	Yes	No
Do you presently have a home air conditioning system?	86	114
If you have a system, would you be interested in upgrading it?	34	52
If you do not have a system, are you interested in purchasing one?	62	52

72. Based on the results of the survey, how many of the 3,000 families identified as potential customers would be interested in purchasing a new unit or upgrading their current one?

    a. 860
    b. 1,290
    c. 1,440
    d. 1,962

73. What percent of the people who have an air conditioning unit in their homes would be interested in upgrading their unit?

    a. 50%
    b. 34%
    c. 40%
    d. 24%

74. The Arctic Blast system costs $1,279.00 and Polar Bear Air Conditioning charges $750.00 to install the system. If sales tax is 6%, what is the total cost for one air conditioning unit including installation?

    a. $2,029.00
    b. $2,105.74
    c. $2,074.00
    d. $2,150.74

75. At Carlos Beltran Day, the Mets decide to give a free Carlos Beltran Bobblehead Doll to every 20th fan who enters Shea Stadium and a free Carlos Beltran jersey to every 125th fan who enters Shea Stadium. The game is a sellout which means that 55,601 fans enter Shea Stadium. How many fans receive the free Carlos Beltran merchandise?

    a. 444
    b. 2,780
    c. 3,113
    d. 3,224

76. Lisa's new cellular phone plan costs $39.99 per month plus $.15 per minute and $.25 per text message. As part of the plan, she gets 250 free minutes and 10 free text messages. If she talked for a total of 5 1/2 hours and sent 32 text messages in her last billing cycle, what were her total charges, before tax?

    a. $56.79
    b. $57.49
    c. $90.49
    d. $94.29

77. In an election for Student Government President, Tasia won 70% of the votes. Her opponent, Rosy, won the rest of the votes. How many votes did Rosy receive if Tasia won 350 votes?

    a. 140
    b. 150
    c. 175
    d. 180

24

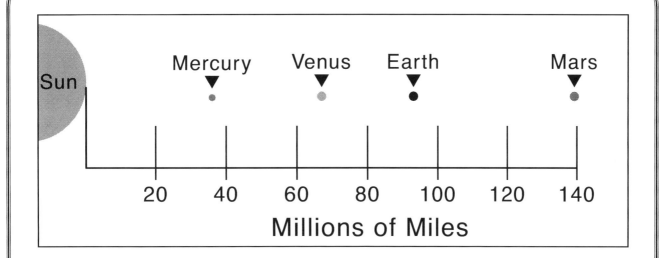

The above diagram shows the distances of the first four planets from the sun.

78. Which of the following would be a reasonable estimate of the distance from the Earth to the sun based on the information in the diagram?

    a. 65 million miles
    b. 95 million miles
    c. 83 million miles
    d. 116 million miles

79. Which two planets are closest to each other?

    a. Mars and Mercury
    b. Venus and Earth
    c. Mercury and Earth
    d. Venus and Mars

80. In Goldville, if three out of every eight residents live in a condo, how many of the 33,000 residents DO NOT live in a condo?

    a. 12,375
    b. 16,500
    c. 20,625
    d. 24,750

81. If the ratio of dogs to cats in a pet store is 5 to 3 and there are 12 cats, how many dogs are there?

    a. 7
    b. 10
    c. 14
    d. 20

Louis was just hired to work as an advertising executive for a magazine. Three days each week he will meet with clients so he decides to buy four new suits. He notices the following ads in the local newspaper.

Suit Warehouse	Scott's Suits	Executive Fashion
ALL SUITS $279.99 Buy 3 Get 1 Free	**Each Suit** $219.99 Everyday Low Price	**Each Suit** $259.99 20% off Total Purchase

82. Where should Louis go to get the best deal? When solving this problem, be sure to show all your work.

---

83. Solve for x:

$$\frac{3}{10} = \frac{x}{35}$$

84. If the ratio of the length of $\overline{WX}$ to the length of $\overline{YZ}$ is 2 to 7 and WX = 24 cm, find the length of $\overline{YZ}$.

Write each verbal phrase as an equation or inequality.

85. Four more than the product of sixteen and n is one hundred.

86. Three less than the sum of seven plus m is greater than five.

87. A number, y, decreased by the sum of nine and the square of x is ten.

88. The quotient of thirty-one and p is less than or equal to eight.

89. Fifteen multiplied by fifty divided by n is seventy-two.

90. Ninety-three divided by the product of fourteen and b is one.

91. One-half of the difference of twenty and z is greater than zero.

92. Double the difference of the square of n and four is equal to n to the fourth power.

Use the Very Berry Punch recipe to solve the problems below.

> **Very Berry Fruit Punch**
> **Recipe Makes 20 Servings**
>
> 3 cups cranberry juice
> 1 1/3 cups grape juice
> 2 2/3 cups pineapple juice
> 2 1/2 pints orange juice
> 2 quarts rainbow sherbet
> 2 1/2 quarts club soda

93. The recipe calls for 2 1/2 quarts of club soda. How many cups of club soda is this?

94. How many cups of pineapple juice would you need to make 90 servings of punch?

95. If the recipe makes 20 servings, calculate the serving size, in ounces.

96. How many half-gallon punch bowls would be needed to hold 120 servings of punch?

97. You decide to buy one-gallon bottles of orange juice. How many would you need to make 360 servings of punch?

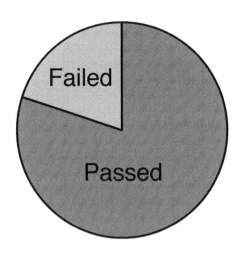

98. One hundred forty algebra students took Ms. Giudici's final exam. Her students' results are shown in the pie chart above. Determine a REASONABLE ESTIMATE of how many students passed this exam.

100. Blaise Pascal created what has become known as Pascal's Triangle pictured below. Fill in the next three rows of the triangle.

```
        1
      1   1
    1   2   1
  1   3   3   1
1   4   6   4   1
```

99. Darci got a new job in a different department so her pay was cut from $780.00 per week to $720.00 per week. Calculate the percent decrease in her salary.

101. Jen scored an 85 on her first math test of the semester. On her next test she scored a 93. Calculate the percent increase of her score.

At Uncle Tony's Used Cars, they sell convertibles, sedans, trucks, SUVs and vans. The pie chart gives the percent of total sales of each type of car in 2004. The sales of SUVs in 2004 totaled $12,840,950. When solving the following problems, be sure to show all your work and explain how you arrived at your answer.

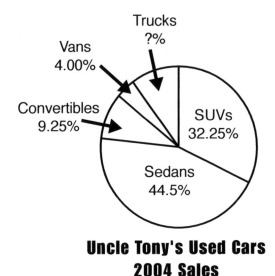

**Uncle Tony's Used Cars
2004 Sales**

102. What was the total amount of sales in 2004?

103. As SUV sales have increased, van sales have fallen. In 2003, the total dollar amount of van sales was $16,460,327. Calculate the percent decrease in van sales from 2003 to 2004.

104. Bob earns $200.00 per week plus $175.00 for every car he sells. In 2003, he received a $5,000.00 bonus as Uncle Tony's Salesperson of the Year. What was his yearly income in 2003, before deductions, if he sold 322 cars?

Enlarged Section

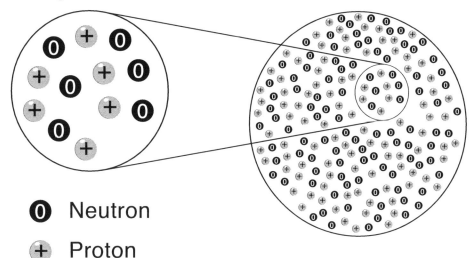

⓪ Neutron

⊕ Proton

Einsteinium Nucleus

105. Einsteinium is an element discovered in 1952 and named for famous scientist Albert Einstein. You are trying to determine the atomic number for Einsteinium. The atomic number is the number of protons or positively charged particles in an atom's nucleus. A diagram of the nucleus of Einsteinium is shown above. Based on the number of protons in the enlarged section, estimate the number of protons in the entire nucleus. When solving this problem, be sure to show all your work.

E   D   F

106. In the above diagram, D cuts segment EF into two segments whose ratio is five to eight. If the length of segment EF is 52 centimeters, find the length of segment ED. When solving this problem, be sure to show all your work.

107. Larry puts $2,000.00 in a savings account that pays 3.1% simple interest. Larry estimates that if he makes no deposits or withdrawals, the account will be worth $2,300.00 in three years. The formula for simple earned interest is $I = Prt$ where I = earned interest, P = principle amount (amount originally invested), r = rate as a decimal, and t = time in years. Is Larry accurate? Explain why or why not. If he is inaccurate, how could he adjust his plan in order to have the desired $2,300.00 in his account?

The maximum capacity of the Wolf Den, the Wolfpack's home arena, is 16,530 people. The average attendance at Wolfpack games this season is 13,625 people per game and the average ticket price is $17.50 per ticket. Last season the average attendance was 12,632 and the average ticket price was $16.00 per ticket. The Wolfpack plays 30 home games per season.

108. The number of tickets sold, known as paid attendance, at a recent Wolfpack game was 14,526. What percent of the arena's seating capacity was filled for this game?

109. At halftime, it was announced that 11,235 people actually attended the game. What percent of the people who purchased tickets actually attended?

110. Determine the percent increase in average attendance per game from last season to this season.

111. If the average ticket price is $17.50 and the Wolfpack has played 15 games this season, calculate the total amount of money generated from ticket sales so far this year.

112. If the average attendance remains the same for the rest of the season, how much more revenue will the Wolfpack generate from ticket sales this year compared to last year?

At Lids Inc., there is a special on hats at the end of the month.

LIDS INC.
Buy 3 Hats @ $24.00 each
Get the Fourth Hat for 1/2 Price

113. The end of the month discount is equivalent to what single discount on the four hats? Give your answer as a percent.

114. You are asked to estimate the square root of 70 to the nearest tenth, without using a calculator. Explain the steps you would take and then follow the steps to estimate the square root of 70.

115. Christine, a computer programming consultant for Big Buy Electronics, charges a fixed fee of $60.00 plus $50.00 for each hour that she works. Tara, a computer programming consultant for Computer City Electronics, charges a fixed rate of $70.00 plus $45.00 for each hour that she works. Christine's company advertises that her rates are cheaper. Are they correct? Explain why or why not. When solving this problem, be sure to show all your work.

116. Betsy's eggnog recipe which produces eight servings requires 2 1/2 cups of buttermilk. She is having a holiday party and wants to make enough eggnog for 28 servings. How many cups of buttermilk will Betsy need?

117. The average American drinks about five soft drinks every three days. ABOUT how many soft drinks will the average American drink in a year? Round your answer to the nearest whole number.

John is offered a job selling appliances. He can choose any of the following monthly salary options:

> ## Option 1:
>
> Straight Commission of 15% of his sales
>
> ## Option 2:
>
> $3,000.00 per month and no commission
>
> ## Option 3:
>
> $2,200.00 per month plus commission of 5% of his sales

118. The sales for the previous four months were $20,000.00, $18,000.00, $27,000.00, and $21,000.00 Which option should John take and why? When solving this problem, be sure to show all your work.

Mountain Bike Race Times	
Year	Winning Time (hours:minutes:seconds)
1964	01:02:43
1974	01:00:42
1984	00:58:21
1994	00:55:21
2004	00:52:49
2014	00:48:45

119. The above table gives the winning times of a local mountain bike race from 1964–2014. Use this information to sketch a scatter plot on the grid shown below. Make sure to label your scatter plot.

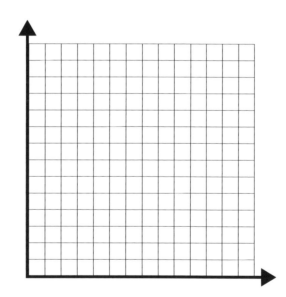

120. Use the information from the table and from your scatter plot to predict what the winning time will be in the year 2024.

37

Yan is trying to decide between a digital cable plan and a satellite dish package. Her job as a consultant is only for two years and she intends to relocate after it ends so she will only live in her apartment for the next two years. The plans of the two companies are shown below:

<table>
<tr>
<td>

Dennis's Digital Cable Service

- **Monthly: $89.99**
- **All 6 Premium Channels:**
  $35.99 per month
- **New Subscriber Bonus:**
  Get 10% off each month's
  bill for the first 6 months

</td>
<td>

Stan's Satellite Service

- **Monthly: $79.99**
- **Premium Channels:**
  $6.49 each per month
- **Special Introductory Offer:**
  Three Premium Channels free
  for the first year.
- **One-Time Set-up Charge:**
  $72.99

</td>
</tr>
</table>

121. Which plan should Yan choose if she wants six premium channels? When solving this problem, be sure to show all your work.

38

On August 28, 1963, Martin Luther King Junior led an estimated 250,000 people in the March on Washington and delivered his famous "I Have a Dream" speech at the Lincoln Memorial. The margin for error of the estimate is 10%. Use the information provided to answer the questions below. Show all work and explain how you arrived at your answers.

122. If the margin for error of the estimate is 10%, how large could the crowd have actually been?

123. How small could the crowd actually have been?

124. If one out of every seven people who participated in the March on Washington was a child, about how many children participated? Round your answer to the nearest whole number.

125. There were 100 members of the United States Congress present at the March on Washington to show support for President Kennedy's Civil Rights Bill. What percent of the crowd did these people represent?

126. During the March on Washington, singers such as Josh White, Odetta, Mahalia Jackson, Joan Baez, and Bob Dylan all performed songs. In how many different orders could they have performed if each singer performed exactly one time?

127. Write the ratio of circles to triangles in the above diagram.

128. How many diamonds would have to be added to make the ratio of diamonds to circles three to one?

129. Greta and eight of her friends go to dinner at a local restaurant. Each entree comes with a salad and the highest priced entree on the menu costs $23.75 while the lowest priced entree costs $19.95. Drinks cost $1.75 each and every person at the table orders one drink. Greta's parents gave her $280.00 to pay for dinner, including the 6% tax and 15% tip. Should $280.00 be enough to cover the entire bill? When solving this problem, be sure to show all your work.

Use the information shown below to solve the following problems.

Irene's Deli
Deli Price List
(prices given per pound)

Ham	$5.29
Roast Beef	$4.59
Bologna	$4.19
Turkey	$4.89
American Cheese	$3.29
Swiss Cheese	$2.89
Cheddar Cheese	$3.49
Mozzarella Cheese	$3.39
Hard Rolls	$.69 each

130. Joe shops at Irene's Deli to buy enough meat to make lunches for himself and his family for the week. He wants to purchase 1 1/2 pounds of ham, 1 3/4 pounds of turkey and 1 3/4 pounds of American Cheese. What is the total weight, in pounds, of his order?

131. Joe decides to buy 20 hard rolls along with his order from the above problem. What is the total amount of his purchase?

132. If ham is on sale for $4.79 per pound, calculate the percent decrease in price per pound.

133. Sneaker Warehouse has a sale on the pair of sneakers that you want. They regularly sell for $69.99 but this week they are on sale for 10% off. The Great American Shoe Store is also having a sneaker sale. They have the same pair of sneakers that regularly cost $81.99 but are on sale for 20% off. You are at the mall trying to decide which pair of sneakers to buy. Estimate the cost of each pair. Based on your estimate, where should you buy the sneakers? When solving this problem, be sure to show all your work.

134. Sean hears a woodpecker and a robin chirping outside his window. Both birds start chirping at the the same time. If the woodpecker chirps every 6 seconds and the robin chirps every 15 seconds, how many times do they chirp together in the first minute he hears them?

135. David wants to take some friends to a baseball game. He plans to sit in the bleachers where tickets cost $22.00 per person. How many friends can he take to the game if he has $210.00?

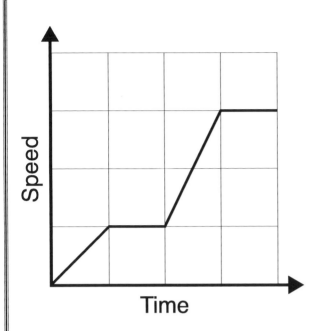

Speed

Time

136. The above graph shows a car's speed over the course of a trip. Which statement BEST describes its speed?

   a. The car's speed increased at a constant rate during the trip.
   b. The car's speed remained the same during the trip.
   c. The car's speed increased at a constant rate, and then it remained the same. It increased again, and then it decreased at a constant rate.
   d. The car's speed increased at a constant rate, and then it remained the same. It increased again at a greater rate, and then it again remained the same.

137. Giovanni drove to college in 4.5 hours. He drove an average of 65 miles per hour on the highway and an average of 25 miles per hour on rural roads. Let h equal the number of hours Giovanni drove on rural roads. Which equation can be used to find his total distance driven?

   a. $65(4.5 - h) + 25h$
   b. $65(4.5) + 25h$
   c. $65h + 25(4.5 - h)$
   d. $65(h - 4.5) + 25h$

138. You and your friends go to a bookstore to buy SAT books on sale for $11.00 each. Together, you spend $138.60, which includes a tax of $6.60. Which equation can be solved to determine how many SAT books, n, you and your friends bought?

   a. $11n - 6.60 = 138.60$
   b. $n = (138.60 + 6.60) \div 11$
   c. $11n = 138.60 + 6.60$
   d. $11n + 6.60 = 138.60$

139. A function is a set of ordered pairs (x, y) that can be described by a rule that creates a one-to-one correspondence between sets of input and output values. In other words, for each input, there is exactly one output. Which input-output table does NOT represent a function?

a.

Input	Output
1	5
2	10
3	15
4	20

c.

Input	Output
2	8
5	15
8	22
11	1

b.

Input	Output
2	9
5	16
9	9
11	23

d.

Input	Output
1	2
2	4
2	6
4	8

140. The cheerleading team ordered tank tops to sell for a fundraiser. The team paid $462.00 for the tops and will sell them for $13.00 each. Which function represents the relationship between the number of tank tops sold, n, and the team's profit?

    a. f(n) = 13n - 462
    b. $f(n)$ = 13n
    c. $f(n)$ = 13n + 462
    d. $f(n)$ = 462n + 13

142. Plane tickets to San Diego cost $400.00 for an economy class ticket and $750.00 for a first class ticket. Ticket sales totaled $81,800.00 and 194 paying passengers were on the plane. How many first class tickets were sold?

    a. 12
    b. 28
    c. 35
    d. 182

141. It costs $3.00 to park at the mall for five hours and $6.00 for each additional hour. Which equation represents the total cost, T, of parking for n hours if $n \geq 5$?

    a. $T = 6n - 2$
    b. $T = 3 + 6(n - 5)$
    c. $T = 3 + 6n$
    d. $T = 6(n - 5)$

143. What is the y-intercept of the function $7x + 3y = 42$?

    a. 42
    b. -7/3
    c. 14
    d. -7

Minutes over 300	Total Cost
0	$30
10	$34
20	$38
35	$44
50	$50

144. The above table shows the cost of a cell phone bill based on the number of minutes over 300 minutes used per month. Which equation represents the function shown in the table.

    a. $y = .4x + 30$
    b. $y = x + 30$
    c. $y = .4x$
    d. $y = 3.4x$

145. If $f(x) = 2/3x - 3$, which of the following ordered pairs does NOT lie on its graph?

    a. $(3, -1)$
    b. $(-6, -7)$
    c. $(12, 11)$
    d. $(0, -3)$

146. Which line below is perpendicular to the line $y = -2/5x + 3$?

    a. $y = -5/2x + 1$
    b. $y = 5/2x$
    c. $y = -2/5x - 3$
    d. $y = 2/5x -3$

46

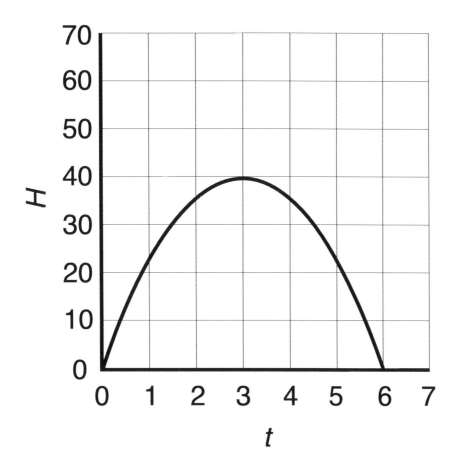

147. A tennis ball is hit with an initial upward velocity of 24 feet per second. The function graphed above, $H = 24t - 4t^2$, where H is the height in feet and t is the time in seconds, describes the height of the ball. Which of the following is the BEST conclusion about the tennis ball's height?

    a. The tennis ball reached its maximum height after about 3 seconds.
    b. The tennis ball's maximum height was 35 feet.
    c. The tennis ball picked up speed as it descended.
    d. The tennis ball returned to the ground in 4 seconds.

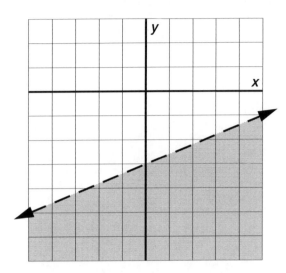

148. Which inequality is represented by the graph?

    a. $y < -2/5x - 3$
    b. $y < 2/5x - 3$
    c. $y < -3x - 2/5$
    d. $y > 2/5x - 3$

150. Debbie needs to grow at least 80 flowers for a flower show. To do so, she is growing roses and sunflowers in her garden. If one rose plant yields 12 flowers and one sunflower plant yields 3 flowers, then the inequality $12x + 3y \geq 80$ represents possible solutions to her problem. Which of the following ordered pairs is a reasonable number of rose and sunflower plants Debbie could grow to have enough flowers for the show?

    a. (2, 17)
    b. (4, 10)
    c. (5, 7)
    d. (6, 2)

149. The equations of two lines are $2x - 5y = 15$ and $y = 2/5x + 1$. Which of the following describes their point of intersection?

    a. (5, 3)
    b. (0, 1)
    c. (10, 5)
    d. no intersection

151. Which of the following is NOT a function?

    a. $y = x$
    b. $y = |x|$
    c. $y = 2x + 10$
    d. $x = y^2$

152. Which graph represents the solution set of the linear inequality $x - y > 2$?

a.

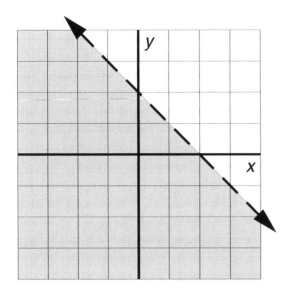

c.

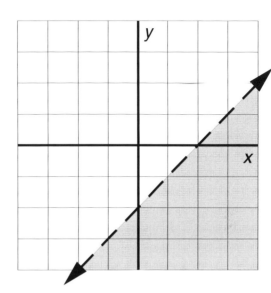

b.

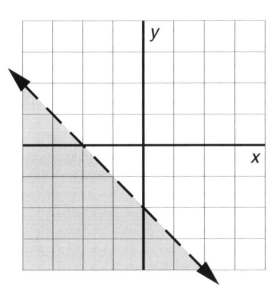

d.

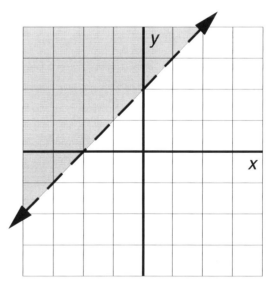

49

153. A mother is twice as old as her daughter. Sixteen years ago she was four times as old as her daughter was then. Which system of linear equations could be used to find the mother's current age, m, and the daughter's current age, d?

   a. $m = 2d$ and $m = 4d + 48$
   b. $m = 2d$ and $m - 16 = 4(d - 16)$
   c. $m = 2d$ and $m - 16 = 4d$
   d. $m = 2d$ and $m = 4(d - 16)$

155. A ball is dropped from an altitude of 200 meters. The equation $h = 200 - 5.1t^2$ describes the height of ball in terms of t seconds. Which is the independent quantity in the function?

   a. The initial altitude, 200 meters
   b. 5.1 meters per second
   c. The height of the ball, h.
   d. The number of seconds, t.

154. If the value of c, in this case 3, in the function of $y = x^2 + 3$ is changed to -3, what is the effect on the graph?

   a. It is translated down three units.
   b. It is reflected over the x-axis.
   c. It is translated up three units.
   d. It is translated down six units.

156. Which of the following lines is parallel to the line $y = 6x - 1$?

   a. $y = -6x + 1$
   b. $y = 1/6x + 1$
   c. $y = -1/6x + 1$
   d. $y = 6x + 1$

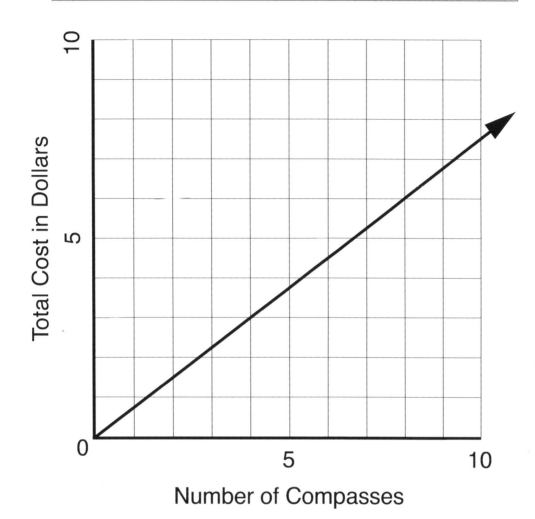

157. A geometry teacher is trying to buy flat compasses for her class. The graph above shows the total cost of compasses as a function of number purchased. Approximately, how much will it cost to purchase 25 compasses?

a. $16.00
b. $17.00
c. $19.00
d. $20.00

158. Which graph below BEST represents the quadratic function $y = 3x^2 - 2$?

a.

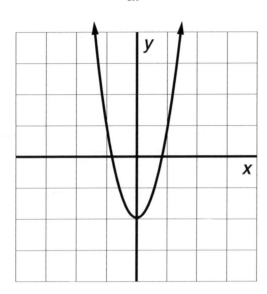

c.

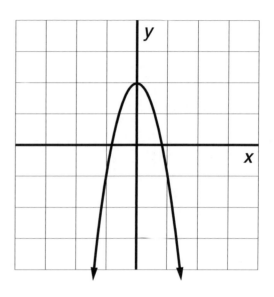

b.

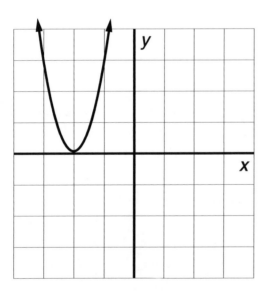

d.

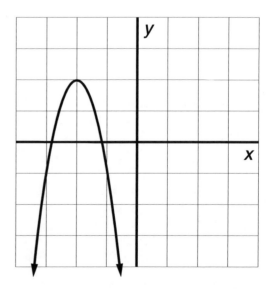

52

Hours	Cost
4	$300
5	$375
7	$525

159. The cost of renting a reception hall is a function of the length of time of the rental. The cost of three rentals is shown in the table. The information is graphed with cost on the vertical axis and hours on the horizontal axis. What does the slope represent?

a. the total cost of each rental
b. the total hours possible for a rental
c. a rate of $75.00 per hour
d. a rate of $300.00 per rental

160. If the ordered pair $(3, n)$ belongs to the function $g(x) = x(x + 1) + 4$, then n equals which of the following?

a. 16
b. 14
c. 12
d. 8

161. For the math meet, Mr. B. purchased three pencils for each student and a box of 20 pencils for the judges. This relationship can be expressed by the function $f(x) = 3x + 20$ where x is the number of students. Which is the dependent quantity in the functional relationship?

a. The number of judges
b. The number of pencils purchased
c. The number of students
d. The number of boxes of pencils

162. What is the slope of the line $x = 13$?

a. 0
b. 13
c. -1/13
d. undefined

163. Which graph represents the solution set of the linear inequality $5x + 5y \leq 10$?

a.

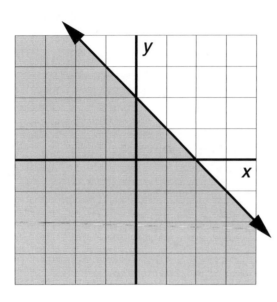

c.

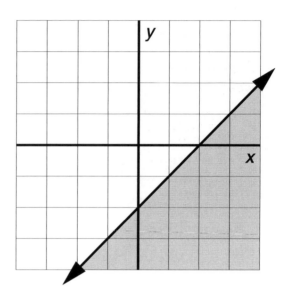

b.

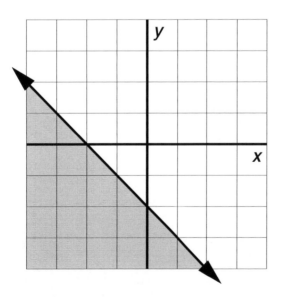

d.

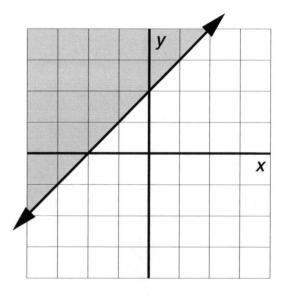

164. In an attempt to break the world record for the largest cup of ice cream, a local ice cream company filled a 1,778-pound metal cup with 450 gallons of ice cream. Which equation expresses w, the total weight of the ice cream and the cup, in terms of x, the average weight of each gallon of ice cream?

a. $w = 450x - 1778$
b. $w = 1778 + 450x$
c. $w = 1778x + 450$
d. $w = 450 - 1778x$

166. Leigh has $35.00 to spend on dessert and balloons for the party. She spends $16.00 on cake and ice cream. If the balloons cost $2.25 each, which inequality models the number of balloons, n, Leigh can buy?

a. $2.25n - 16 \leq 35$
b. $16 - 2.25n \leq 35$
c. $2.25n \leq 35 + 16$
d. $16 + 2.25n \leq 35$

165. If the graph of $y = 2x - 1$ is changed to $y = 5x - 1$, which of the following is NOT true about the resulting graph?

a. It has a y-intercept of -1.
b. Its graph is steeper than the graph of the original function.
c. Its graph is less steep than the graph of the original function.
d. It has a slope of 5.

$$y = 3/4x - 7$$
$$5x + 4y = 4$$

167. What is the solution of the system of linear equations?

a. $(4, -4)$
b. $(0, -7)$
c. $(2, -5.5)$
d. There is no solution.

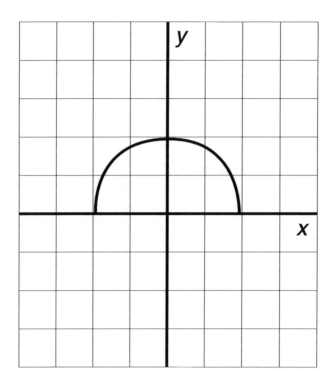

168. Which of the following BEST describes the range represented by the above graph?

    a. $y \geq 0$
    b. $-2 \leq y \leq 2$
    c. $y \leq 2$
    d. $0 \leq y \leq 2$

169. What are the solutions to the equation $x^2 + 7x - 18 = 0$?

    a. {2, 9}
    b. {2, -9}
    c. {-2, -9}
    d. {-2, 9}

170. What is the x-intercept of the graph of $4x - 5y = -36$?

    a. -9
    b. 36/5
    c. 36
    d. 4

171. Which graph represents the solution to the following system of linear equations?

$$y = 1/2x - 3$$
$$9x - 3y = -6$$

a.

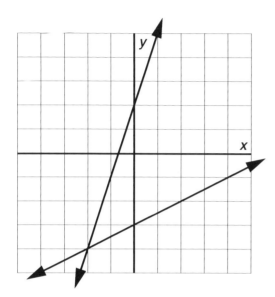

c.

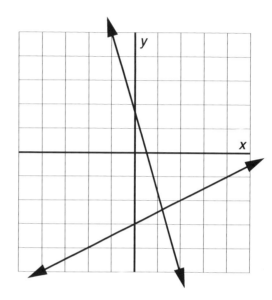

b.

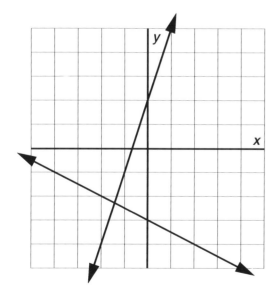

d.

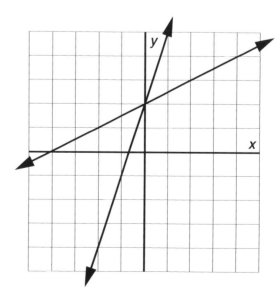

57

172. The net monthly profit that a gym makes on membership dues is represented by the equation: $p = 75n - 12{,}525$, where n is the number of members. Which is the BEST interpretation of this equation?

    a. The gym's profit is greater than $12,525.00
    b. The gym has sold 167 memberships.
    c. The gym makes $12,525.00 profit.
    d. The gym needs to have 168 dues-paying members in order to make a profit.

174. If the coefficient of x^2 in the function $y = -1/2x^2$ is changed to 5, what is the effect on the graph?

    a. The graph becomes narrower.
    b. The graph is reflected across the x-axis.
    c. The graph becomes narrower and is reflected across the x-axis.
    d. The graph becomes wider and is reflected across the x-axis.

$$-x + y = 6$$
$$4x = 4y - 24$$

173. How many solutions does the system of linear equations above have?

    a. one solution
    b. two solutions
    c. infinitely many solutions
    d. no solution

175. What is the equation of the line with a slope of -3 and a y-intercept of 15?

    a. $y = -3x + 15$
    b. $y = 15x + 3$
    c. $y = -3x - 15$
    d. $y = 15x - 3$

58

176. Pam is shipping school supplies, mainly notebooks and dictionaries, to a classmate in Mexico. To get the best shipping rate, each box must weight 15 pounds. If each notebook weighs 0.5 pounds and the each dictionary weighs 3 pounds, which of the following equations represents the number of notebooks, n, and dictionaries, d, that Pam can pack in each box.

    a. $.5n + 3d = 15$
    b. $.5n + d = 15$
    c. $3n + .5d = 15$
    d. $.5n + 15d = 15$

177. Ruth's local video store charges $19.99 per month for a VIP Membership and $1.80 per video rented. If n is the number of videos Ruth rents in a month, what expression can be used to determine the total amount Ruth spent at the video store?

    a. $1.80n + 19.99 = \text{total}$
    b. $19.99n + 1.90 = \text{total}$
    c. $n + 19.99 = \text{total}$
    d. $1.80 + 19.99 = \text{total}$

178. There are 1,960 students who attend high school, 940 of which are boys. At a recent softball championship game at the school, 35% of the female students and 40% of the male students were in attendance. What percent of the crowd at the softball game, rounded to the nearest whole number, was female?

    a. 35%
    b. 40%
    c. 49%
    d. 55%

179. What number appears in the ones place of 3^{53}?

    a. 3
    b. 9
    c. 7
    d. 1

180. At Marie's Candy Shoppe, dark chocolates worth $4.20 per pound are to be mixed with milk chocolates worth $3.20 per pound to create a ten-pound mixture of candy worth $3.90 per pound. How many pounds of dark chocolates must be used?

    a. 6
    b. 6.5
    c. 7
    d. 8

181. The sum of the digits in a two-digit number is 11. When the digits are reversed, the number increases by 27. What is this number?

    a. 38
    b. 47
    c. 71
    d. 74

Jason bought a baseball card whose value increases according to the following formula:

$$V = 125(1.2)^n$$

where n is the number of years since its purchase.

182. If Jason bought the card in 2004, what will be the value of the card in the year 2007?

    a. $216.00
    b. $260.00
    c. $300.00
    d. $450.00

183. During what year will the value of the card reach $500.00?

    a. 2008
    b. 2010
    c. 2012
    d. 2014

184. The vertex of a parabola is either the maximum or minimum value of the graph. The vertex is a maximum if the parabola is concave down and a minimum if the parabola is concave up. The x-coordinate of the vertex is the x value of the maximum or minimum of the function, and the y-coordinate of the vertex is the maximum value of the function. If a quadratic function is in standard form, $y = ax^2 + bx + c$, the maximum or minimum value of the function is the y value when $x = -b/2a$. Which of the following would be the maximum value of the function $f(x) = -4x^2 + 2x + 1$?

a. 4
b. 1/2
c. 1 1/4
d. 2

185. A local high school dance team sold gift wrap to earn money for a trip to Disney World. The gift wrap in solid colors sold for $5.00 per roll, and the print gift wrap sold for $7.00 per roll. The total number of rolls sold was 357, and the total amount of money collected was $2,037.00. How many solid-colored rolls of gift wrap were sold?

a. 95
b. 126
c. 164
d. 231

186. Pat has a part time job at a local flower shop in addition to her full time job as a librarian. She works a total of 48 hours per week and spends three times as many hours at the library as she does at the flower shop. How many hours per week does Pat spend working at the library?

a. 12
b. 24
c. 32
d. 36

MATHEMATICSMATHEMATICSMA....

187. Which of the following would be the 201st letter in the above pattern?

    a. M
    b. A
    c. T
    d. H

188. The roots, or solutions, of a quadratic equation are values of the variable that satisfy the equation. A quadratic equation can have 0, 1, or 2 roots, and the roots are the x values that result when $f(x) = 0$. In other words, the roots are the x-intercepts of the graph of a function or the zeroes of the function. You can also find the roots by factoring the quadratic equation and solving for x. What are the roots of the quadratic equation $x^2 - 5x = 14$

    a. -2 and 2
    b. 7 and -2
    c. 7 and 2
    d. -7 and 2

The number of customers who used the drive-through window at a fast food restaurant between 6:00 p.m. and 10:00 p.m. last week is given below.

Day	Customers
Sunday	57
Monday	63
Tuesday	72
Wednesday	84
Thursday	99
Friday	117

189. Based on the above table, which of the following would be a REASONABLE prediction of the number of customers that used the drive-through on Saturday?

   a. 138
   b. 122
   c. 108
   d. 97

190. A person who weighs 120 pounds burns $108 + x$ calories in one hour of standing and burns three times as many calories in one hour of walking. Which of the following equations can be used to determine how many calories, c, a 120-pound person burns in 45 minutes of walking?

   a. $c = .75(3x + 324)$
   b. $c = .75(3x + 108)$
   c. $c = .75(x + 324)$
   d. $c = .75(3x + 360)$

$$4, -12, 36, -108, 324 \ldots$$

191. Find the seventh term in the above pattern.

   a. -432
   b. -972
   c. 2,916
   d. -8,748

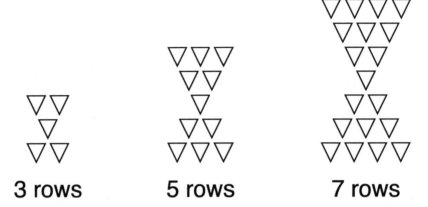

3 rows   5 rows   7 rows

192. How many triangles would be needed to make a model with 45 rows?

    a. 45
    b. 225
    c. 551
    d. 2,025

3, 5, 8, 12, 17, . . .

193. Which of the following would be the tenth number in the above pattern?

    a. 27
    b. 36
    c. 47
    d. 57

194. Which of the following is the equation of the line that passes through points (4, -2) and (3, -11)?

    a. $y = 9x - 38$
    b. $y = 3x + 9$
    c. $y = 9x - 19$
    d. $y = 9x + 38$

Jill saw an ad for a rare coin collection that said the the coin collection triples in value every year. She bought the collection for $60.00 at the end of 1999.

195. What was the value of the coin collection after five years?

    a. $2,700.00
    b. $14,580.00
    c. $43,740.00
    d. $187,500.00

196. If the value of the coin collection does indeed triple every year, when did the value of the coin collection reach $4,000.00?

    a. after 2 years
    b. after 3 years
    c. after 4 years
    d. after 5 years

197. The base of a parallelogram is 5 centimeters less than two times its height. The area of the parallelogram is 12 square centimeters. What is the height of the the parallelogram?

    a. 2 centimeters
    b. 4 centimeters
    c. 6 centimeters
    d. 7 centimeters

198. If Mike placed $1.00 in an account that doubled every day, how much money would be in the account after 19 days?

    a. $19.00
    b. $16,384.00
    c. $262,144.00
    d. $1,048,576.00

The sales during the week of Christmas at a local department store over the past five years are given below.

Year	Sales
2000	$57,564.00
2001	$54,110.00
2002	$51,405.00
2003	$49,348.00
2004	$47,868.00

199. Which of the following would be the MOST REASONABLE prediction for sales for Christmas 2005?

    a. $48,500.00
    b. $47,600.00
    c. $46,900.00
    d. $45,100.00

200. A Florida motel charges a different rate for beachfront and poolside rooms. When 15 beachfront rooms are occupied, the motel collects $2,700.00 When 10 poolside rooms and 10 beachfront rooms are occupied, the motel collects $3,050.00. How much does the motel charge for each poolside room?

    a. $125.00
    b. $180.00
    c. $190.00
    d. $250.00

201. In 1992, a company lost $750,000.00 In 2004, the same company had a profit of $1,200,000.00 Which of the following would be the average rate of change in profit from 1992 to 2004?

    a. $37,500.00 per year
    b. $100,000.00 per year
    c. $162,500.00 per year
    d. $150,000.00 per year

202. A landscaper charges a fee of $55.00 to come to your home plus an hourly rate for labor. The landscaper will work at one house for four hours and charge $121.00 for his work. Let h equal the hourly rate. Which of the following equations would determine the landscaper's hourly rate?

  a. $h - 55 = 121$
  b. $55 = 4h - 121$
  c. $4h + 55 = 121$
  d. $121 + 4h = 55$

203. Which of the following would be the landscaper's hourly rate?

  a. $16.50
  b. $17.50
  c. $17.75
  d. $22.00

204. The amount a spring stretches varies directly with the weight of the object attached to it. A 15-pound weight causes a spring to stretch 24 centimeters. How much weight will stretch the spring eight centimeters?

  a. 3 pounds
  b. 5 pounds
  c. 8 pounds
  d. 12 pounds

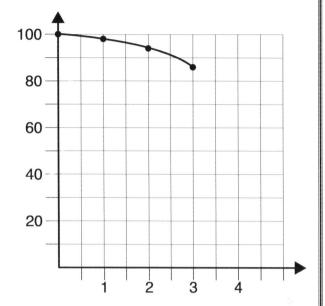

205. Which of the following would MOST LIKELY be the value of y when $x = 4$?

  a. 92
  b. 79
  c. 70
  d. 55

206. For what value of x will $y = 38$?

  a. 5
  b. 6
  c. 7
  d. 8

Mrs. Sylvestre uses three test grades (T_1, T_2, T_3), three quiz grades (Q_1, Q_2, Q_3), and a homework grade (H) to determine each student's grade for the quarter. When computing her grades, Mrs. Sylvestre used the following formula:

$$\frac{3(T_1 + T_2 + T_3) + 2(Q_1 + Q_2 + Q_3) + H}{16}$$

207. A student received grades of 87, 93 and 82 on her three tests, 90, 94, and 88, on her three quizzes and a homework grade of 93. What was her grade for the quarter, rounded to the nearest hundredth?

    a. 88.50
    b. 88.75
    c. 88.94
    d. 89.57

208. Another student missed the third test and must make it up after school. Her test grades are 81 and 75, her quiz grades are 80, 81, and 73, and her homework grade is an 83. She wants to know what grade she must receive in order to earn an 80 for the quarter. What should Mrs. Sylvester tell her?

    a. 80
    b. 83
    c. 87
    d. 90

209. If John's quiz average is an 87 and his homework grade is a 90, what must his test average be in order for his grade to be a 92 for the quarter, rounded to the nearest hundredth?

    a. 92.25
    b. 95.56
    c. 95.89
    d. 96.00

210. They orders food to sell at a breakfast cage. Coffee costs $6.00 per pound and bagels cost $3.50 per dozen. If he plans to spend no more than $55.00 and orders at least one pound of coffee, c, which inequality would represent the number of bagels, b, They can order?

    a. ($3.50/12)$b$ + 6.00c$ ≤ $55.00
    b. $55.00 + ($3.50/12)b > 6.00c$
    c. 6.00c$ - ($3.50/12)$b$ ≥ $55.00
    d. ($3.50/12)$b$ + 6.00c$ ≥ $55.00

211. The admission to a play costs $15.00 for children and $20.00 for adults. On a given day, $5,790.00 is collected and 326 people attend the show. How many of them are children?

    a. 123
    b. 146
    c. 175
    d. 180

212. Tickets for a high school football game cost $3.00 for students and $5.00 for the general public. Ticket sales totaled $1,590.00, and 426 people attended the game. How many student tickets were sold?

    a. 156
    b. 160
    c. 189
    d. 270

Brian works in a science lab. He is studying the rate at which a certain bacterial virus spreads. He placed a sample of the virus in a dish and used a microscope to examine the dish every hour to determine the number of bacteria present. The table below shows Brian's data.

Time	Bacteria Present
10:00 a.m.	45
11:00 a.m.	135
12:00 p.m.	405
1:00 p.m.	1,215

213. If the bacteria continues to grow at the same rate, how many bacteria should be present in the dish by 3:00 p.m.?

    a. 2,430
    b. 3,645
    c. 10,935
    d. 32,805

214. If the bacteria continues to grow at the same rate, at what time will there be 98,415 bacteria present in the dish?

    a. 3 p.m.
    b. 4 p.m.
    c. 5 p.m.
    d. 8 p.m.

$$h(x) = 3 \div (x - 1)$$

215. The domain is the set of all values of the independent variable of a function, and the range is the set of all values of the dependent variable. Which of the following is the domain of the above function.

    a. $x = 1$
    b. $x \neq 1$
    c. $x \neq -1$
    d. $x > 1$

216. The cost of a taxi ride is calculated by adding a fixed amount to a charge for each 1/4 mile of the trip. If a one-mile trip costs $5.00 and a 1 1/2 mile trip costs $6.50, what will be the cost of a three-mile trip?

    a. $8.00
    b. $9.00
    c. $11.00
    d. $14.50

217. Karen had scores of 78, 84, 94, and 76 on her first four algebra tests. What must she score on the next test in order to have an average of at least an 85?

    a. 85
    b. 88
    c. 91
    d. 93

218. The total cost of a laptop is the price of the laptop plus a 5.5% sales tax. If the total cost of the laptop, C, is a function of the price of the laptop, p, which of the following best represents this information?

    a. $C = p + .055p$
    b. $C = p + 5.5p$
    c. $C = 1 + .055p$
    d. $C = p - .055p$

One way to solve a quadratic equation, $y = ax^2 + bx + c$, is to use the Quadratic Formula:

$$X = \frac{-b \pm \sqrt{b^2 - 4ac}}{2a}$$

219. Which of the following would be the solution(s) to the equation $y = x^2 - 5x + 6$?

    a. $x = 3$, or $x = -2$
    b. $x = 3$
    c. $x = 6$, or $x = 4$
    d. $x = 3$, or $x = 2$

220. Danny rents a moving van by the hour. He pays a $25.00 fee and $10.00 for each hour he uses the van. Let T represent the total cost of renting the van for h hours. Which of the following equations represents the dependent variable in terms of the independent variable?

    a. $T = 25 + 10h$
    b. $h = T/10 - 2.5$
    c. $T = 25 - 10h$
    d. $h = T - 25$

221. Claire is planting a garden that must be five feet longer than it is wide. The garden must be at least 15 feet wide and no more than 22 feet wide. The function $f(w) = w(w+5)$ describes the area of the garden in terms of its width, w, in feet. What is the range of this function?

    a. range = 15 feet to 22 feet
    b. range = 300 square feet to 594 square feet
    c. range = 20 feet to 27 feet
    d. range = 500 square feet to 864 square feet

222. What number appears in the ones place of 7^{26}?

    a. 7
    b. 9
    c. 3
    d. 1

223. With prom season approaching, a wholesaler is offering two different package deals to local florists. One package contains 30 dozen roses and 24 dozen stargazer lillies and costs $594.00. The other package contains 15 dozen roses and 10 dozen stargazer lillies and costs $285.00. What is the price of a dozen roses?

a. $0.50
b. $6.00
c. $7.50
d. $15.00

3, 9, 15, 21, 27, . . .

225. What would be the sixteenth number in the above pattern?

a. 87
b. 90
c. 93
d. 99

224. In 2006, Sarah's salary was $10,000.00 less than twice the salary of Jen. If j represents Jen's salary and s represents Sarah's salary in 2006, which expression can be used to determine Jen's salary?

a. $j = s - 10,000$
b. $s = j + 10,000$
c. $j = s/2 + 5,000$
d. $s = 2j - 5,000$

226. Which of the following represents the linear function that contains the points (-5, 15) and (10, 24) in slope-intercept form?

a. $y = 9x + 15$
b. $y = 3/5x - 18$
c. $y = 3x + 15$
d. $y = 3/5x + 18$

There are two gyms in Fairfield. Copies of their ads are shown below.

Fairfield Gym

$379.00 per year for the
first family member
plus
$139.00 per year for each
additional family member

Physique Plus

$439.00 per year for the
first family member
plus
$109.00 per year for each
additional family member

227. Which equation shows the cost for a family with x members at the Fairfield Gym?

   a. Total Cost = $379.00 + $139.00($x$ - 1)
   b. Total Cost = $379.00 + 139.00x$
   c. Total Cost = $379.00 - $139.00($x$ - 1)
   d. Total Cost = 379.00x$ - 139.00x$

228. Which equation shows the cost for a family with x members at Physique Plus?

   a. Total Cost = $109.00($x$ - 1) - $439.00
   b. Total Cost = $439.00 + 109.00x$
   c. Total Cost = $439.00($x$ - 1) + $109.00($x$ - 1)
   d. Total Cost = $439.00 + $109.00($x$ - 1)

229. How many family members can join either gym for which the cost of joining either gym would be equal?

   a. 3
   b. 4
   c. 5
   d. 7

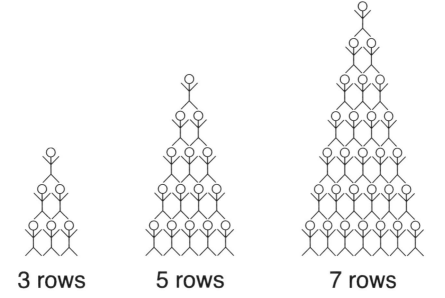

3 rows   5 rows   7 rows

230. Continuing the above pattern, how many people would be in a pyramid of fifteen rows?

   a. 105
   b. 120
   c. 130
   d. 136

231. The dance club members must raise at least $150.00 for a field trip to a salsa performance in the city. To do so, they are selling candy bars for $2.00 each and lollipops for $0.50 each. Which of the following inequalities represents the number of candy bars, b, and the number of lollipops, p, that the club must sell?

   a. $2b + .5p \geq 150$
   b. $.5b + 2p > 150$
   c. $2b + .5p < 150$
   d. $2b - .5p > 150$

$$C = S + .10(M - 200) + .25T$$

George's cellular phone company calculates his monthly bill using the above formula where S is the base price per month of \$39.99, M is the number of minutes spent on the phone, T is the number of text messages sent, and C is the total dollar amount of the bill.

232. In March, George spent a total of 297 minutes on the phone and sent 23 text messages. What was his total bill in March?

    a. \$95.44
    b. \$57.84
    c. \$49.69
    d. \$55.44

233. If George's total bill for April was \$57.99 and he sent 24 text message, how many minutes did he spend talking on the phone in April?

    a. 240
    b. 260
    c. 290
    d. 320

234. If George spent 457 minutes on the phone in May and his bill was \$83.69, how many text messages did he send in June?

    a. 36
    b. 56
    c. 72
    d. 108

The yearly internet sales for a company over the past ten years are given in the graph below.

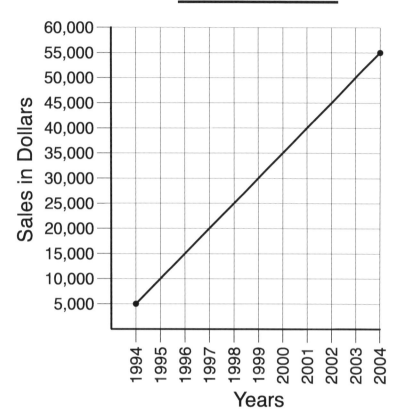

Internet Sales

235. Using this information, which of the following would be the BEST prediction of the total internet sales for the year 2010?

    a. $85,000.00
    b. $90,000.00
    c. $100,000.00
    d. $80,000.00

Expense	Cost
Airfare	$900.00
Hotel Room	$25.00 daily
Meals	$40.00 daily
Transportation	$450.00
Miscellaneous	$375.00

236. Rose saved $2,720.00 for a trip to Florence, Italy. She budgeted the expenses, as shown in the above table. What is the GREATEST number of days Rose can stay in Florence, assuming she cannot exceed $2,720.00 in expenses?

   a. 7
   b. 15
   c. 16
   d. 23

1, 1, 2, 3, 5, 8, 13, 21, . . .

237. The Fibonacci sequence is shown above. Which of the following are the next three terms in the sequence?

   a. 34, 55, 93
   b. 32, 45, 60
   c. 34, 55, 89
   d. 39, 72, 132

238. What is the slope of the function $4y = -2x + 16$?

   a. -2
   b. -1/2
   c. 2
   d. -4

The chart below shows the number of degrees in a polygon.

Shape	Number of Sides	Total Degrees
Triangle	3	180°
Quadrilateral	4	360°
Pentagon	5	540°
Hexagon	6	720°
Heptagon	7	900°
Decagon	10	????

239. How many degrees are there in a decagon?

    a. 1,080°
    b. 1,260°
    c. 1,440°
    d. 1,620°

240. The graph of $y = x^2 + 1$ is translated 8 units up and reflected across the x-axis. What would be the equation of the new graph?

    a. $y = x^2 + 9$
    b. $y = -x^2 - 9$
    c. $y = x^2 - 8$
    d. $x = y^2 - 8$

241. The function $y = 4x - 10$ is changed to $y = 4x + 2$. What is the effect on the graph of the function?

    a. The graph moves left 8 units.
    b. The graph moves down 12 units.
    c. The graph moves up 12 units.
    d. The graph moves right 10 units.

79

○△□○○△△□□○○○△△△□□□○○○○

242. Which of the following would be the 100th shape in the above pattern?

    a. ○

    b. △

    c. □

    d. ▱

243. Aaliyah owns a tie shop in Manhattan. She has been selling 300 ties per week at a price of $35.00 per tie. She finds that for every $2.00 she drops the price of the ties she can sell 60 more ties per week. At what price should she sell the ties in order to maximize her weekly sales?

    a. $29.00
    b. $27.00
    c. $23.00
    d. $15.00

Figure A

Figure B

Figure C

244. How many dots will be in Figure H if it follows the pattern shown above?

    a. 100
    b. 89
    c. 81
    d. 64

245. Which of the following would be the solution(s) to the equation $5x^2 + 18x - 8 = 0$?

    a. -18 and 22
    b. 2/5 and -4
    c. 5 and 10
    d. 4 and 36

246. The y-intercept of a line is the point where $x = 0$. Similarly, the x-intercept is the point where $y = 0$. What are the x and y intercepts of the line $2x - 6y = 12$.

    a. (0, -6) and (2, 0)
    b. (0, -2) and (6, 0)
    c. (0, 6) and (-2, 0)
    d. (0, -12) and (-6, 0)

Carole and Jim both work at the Meadows selling promotional items during concerts. Carole works for PRO T-Shirts and sells T-shirts for $10.00 each. She earns $40.00 per game plus $1.50 for each shirt that she sells. Jim works for EXPECT Discount T-Shirt Company and sells T-shirts for $12.00 each. He earns $35.00 per game plus $2.00 for each T-shirt he sells.

247. Write an equation that describes Carole's salary per game, S, as a function of the number of T-shirts she sells, n.

$S = 40 + 1.50n$

Day	T-Shirts Sold
Monday	22
Wednesday	15
Friday	35
Saturday	40

248. Use the information in the above chart to determine how much money Carole made last week.

249. Write an equation that describes Jim's salary per game, S, as a function of the number of T-shirts he sells.

250. How many T-shirts did Jim sell at Saturday's game if he made $109.00?

251. How many T-shirts would Carole and Jim have to sell to each earn the same salary for working one game? When solving this problem, be sure to show all your work.

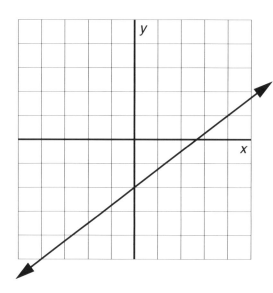

$$V < \wedge > V < \wedge > \ldots$$

254. Identify the 79th shape in the above pattern.

252. What is the slope of the line graphed above?

253. Find the equation of the line with a *y*-intercept of (0, -2) and an *x*-intercept of (3, 0). Write your answer in slope-intercept form.

255. What number appears in the 54th decimal place of 7/11?

Amanda bought a new boat for $32,500.00. Her insurance agent tells her that the boat's value will depreciate by 15% of its value in the previous year for each of the next two years. In each of the next four years, the boat's value will depreciate by 8% of its value the previous year.

256. Sketch a graph of the value, V of the boat in terms of years from purchase, t.

257. What is the value of the boat two years after Amanda purchases it?

258. If value of the boat depreciates as described above, by what percent will its value have decreased after four years? When solving this problem, be sure to show all your work.

259. Amanda plans to sell her boat when its value drops below $18,000.00. What is the minimum number of full years from the date of purchase that the boat will have a value below $18,000.00?

84

x	y
1	3
2	6
3	11
4	18

260. The table above shows a functional relationship between x and y. Write a rule to represent the function.

262. Ms. Shea decided to invest money earned from an inheritance. She invested $10,000 at an annual rate of 5% and the rest of the money, n, at an annual rate of 7.2%. Write an equation to describe, I, the total amount of interest earned from both investments during the first year.

.341534153415. . .

261. What number would appear in the 57th place of the repeating decimal shown above?

263. A swimming pool is composed of 4% chlorine. The rest of the pool is pure water. If the lifeguard drains x gallons out of the pool, write an equation to represent w, the number of gallons of water he drained.

Kathleen's French teacher scaled the last test set of quizzes by adding the same number of points to each student's grade. All questions on the quiz were worth the same number of points. Kathleen received a scaled score of 88% and had 17 questions correct, while Chris received a scaled score of 63% and had 12 questions correct.

264. Write an equation to calculate the scaled test scores from the number of questions correct, n.

265. Describe the slope and y-intercept of the equation.

266. Draw a graph of the function.

267. If Emily had 15 correct answers on the quiz, what would be her scaled grade?

A small plane takes off from an airport and reaches an altitude of 4,000 feet after ten minutes. For the next 1.5 hours, the plane remains at an altitude between 5,000 feet and 3,500 feet. Finally the plane descends at a rate of 80 feet per minute.

268. Sketch a graph on the grid below to represent the flight path of the small plane. Use height as a function of time. Remember to title the graph and label the axes.

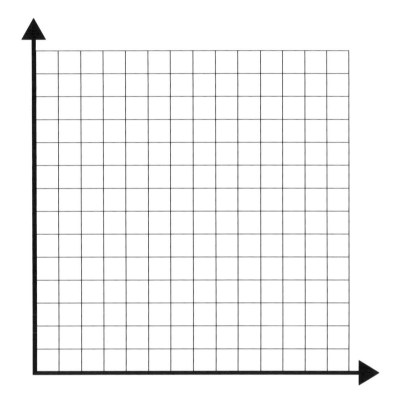

269. Approximately how long was the flight? When solving this problem, be sure to show all your work.

270. The population of a certain town rose steadily from 1980 to 1990, remained constant from 1990 through 1995, then declined sharply from 1995–1998, then remained constant until 2003. Sketch a graph that represents the situation described above. Be sure to label the axes.

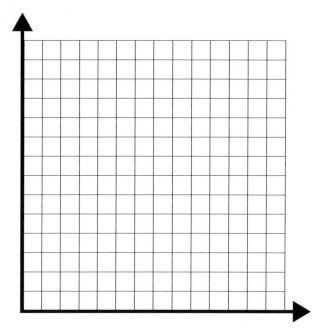

271. Marris designs and maintains web sites for local businesses. She charges $160.00 for a consultation plus $90.00 for each hour she spends designing and maintaining the web site. A new web consultant has opened a business in the area and he charges $100.00 plus $95.00 for each hour he spends designing and maintaining the web site. The new web consultant advertises that his rates are cheaper. Is the new web consultant correct? Explain your reasoning.

272. Graph $y < x + 1$.

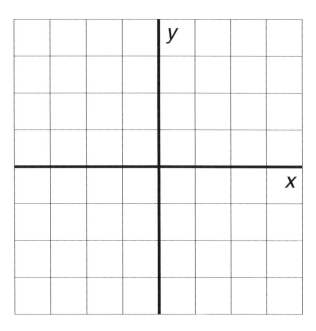

5, 12, 19, 26, 33, . . .

273. Find the twelfth number in the above pattern.

274. The length of a field is 8 more than twice its width. The area is 64 square yards. Find the dimensions of the field. When solving this problem, be sure to show all your work.

89

Students agreed to hold a fund raiser for their senior class trip to Disney World. Members of the class council were presented with two fund raising options: a car wash, and a candy sale. A local gas station has offered to let them use their facilities on Saturday so if they hold the car wash, they would only have to pay for supplies which the class advisors estimated would cost $150.00. They would sell tickets to the car wash for $7.00 each. If they sell candy, they make $5.00 for each case of 20 candy bars that they sell.

275. Write an equation for the profit the class would make at the car wash, P, in terms of the number of cars that they wash, c.

276. Write an equation for the profit the class would make by holding a candy sale, P, in terms of the number of cases of candy bars they sell, c.

277. Write and solve an equation that shows the number of items that would need to be sold so that the profit is the same for both car wash tickets and cases of candy bars.

278. If you were on the class council, which of the fundraisers would you vote to hold? Show your work or explain your reasoning.

90

The local phone company offers three different plans for long distance calls:

Plan 1:	Plan 2:	Plan 3:
$39.99 per month plus $.10 per minute	$35.99 per month plus $.15 per minute	$74.99 per month with unlimited local calls

279. Write an equation for the cost C, of long distance phone service in a given month for Plan 1 in terms of the minutes spent talking, m.

280. Write an equation for the cost C, of long distance phone service in a given month for Plan 2 in terms of the minutes spent talking, m.

281. Write an equation for the cost C, of long distance phone service in a given month for Plan 3 in terms of the minutes spent talking, m.

January	350
February	375
March	365
April	360
May	357

282. Terra's long distance minutes for the last five months are listed above. Which plan should she choose? When solving this problem, be sure to show all your work.

The population of Splitsville has been decreasing by approximately the same percent each year. The table below shows the town's population over the past five years.

Year	Population
1999	25,004
2000	22,005
2001	19,362
2002	17,036
2003	14,992

283. By what percent has the population of Splitsville decreased each year? Show your work or explain how you arrived at your answer.

284. If this rate of decrease continues, what will be Splitsville's approximate population in 2008? When solving this problem, be sure to show all your work.

285. The roots, or solutions, of a quadratic equation are values of the variable that satisfy the equation. A quadratic equation can have 0, 1, or 2 roots, and the roots are the x values that result when $f(x) = 0$. In other words, the roots are the x-intercepts of the graph of a function or the zeroes of the function. You can also find the roots by factoring the quadratic equation and solving for x. Find the roots of $y = x^2 - 5x + 6$.

286. Michael is trying to gain weight to start the wrestling season. His coach has placed him on a diet in order to consume 1,200 extra calories a day. Mike's protein shakes have 330 calories each and his snack bars have 180 calories each. Write an equation to represent the number of shakes, s, and bars, b, that Mike should eat each day for his diet.

287. The football booster club spends $500.00 a month to maintain its hotdog concession stand. If hot dogs cost $0.50 to make and are sold for $3.75, how many hotdogs must the club sell each month to make a profit of $1,502.00 per month?

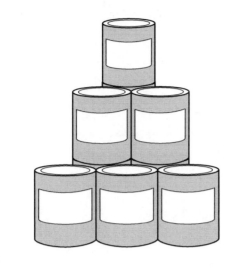

289. The length of a picture frame is 2 less than 3 times the width. The area of the frame is 16 square inches. Find the dimensions of the picture. When solving this problem, be sure to show all your work.

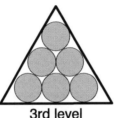

1st level   2nd level   3rd level

288. At a local grocery store, you are responsible for building a display in the showcase. How many cans of soup will you need to build a nine-level model if you used ten cans to form a three-level model as shown in the above diagram?

4, 8/3, 16/9, 32/27, 64/81, . . .

290. Find the eighth term in the above pattern.

A local convenience store sells orange juice in half-pint (8 ounces), pint (16 ounces), quart (32 ounces) and half-gallon (64 ounces) containers. The prices are given below.

Container	Price
Half-Pint	$.99
Pint	$1.29
Quart	$1.89
Half-Gallon	$2.49

The equation that approximates the relationship in the above table is

$$P = .03N + .75$$

where P = the price of the orange juice and N = the number of ounces of orange juice in the container.

291. Explain the meaning of the .03 in the equation.

292. Explain the meaning of the .75 in the equation.

293. Based on the graph and the equation, predict the price of a gallon of orange juice. When solving this problem, be sure to show all your work.

294. Sketch a graph that illustrates the relationship between the number of people painting a house and the amount of time it takes to complete the job. Be sure to label the axes.

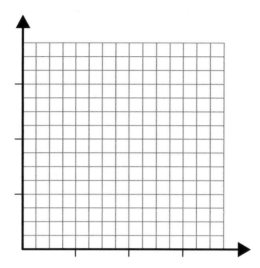

4, 16, 64, 256, 1024, . . .

295. Find the next three terms in the above pattern. Explain how you reached your answer.

296. What is the slope of the line passing through the points (12, -9) and (-3, -4)?

A bungee jumper leaps off of a bridge 90 yards above water. Her height, B after t seconds is given by the following function:

$$B(t) = 90 - 6.2t^2$$

297. How far from the water will the bungee jumper be after two seconds?

298. How long will it take her to hit the water?

299. Sketch a graph that gives the height, B, of the bungee jumper during the first three seconds on the grid provided.

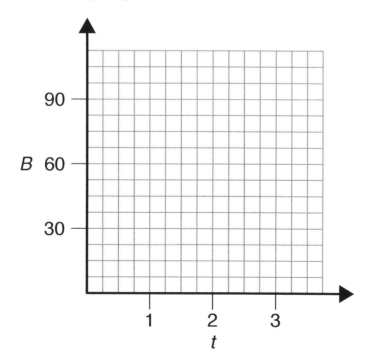

The table below shows the cost of producing purses.

Number of Purses	2	4	6	8	10
Cost	$44	$68	$92	$116	$140

300. On the grid provided, sketch a line graph of the data in the chart above with cost, C, expressed as a function of purses produced, p.

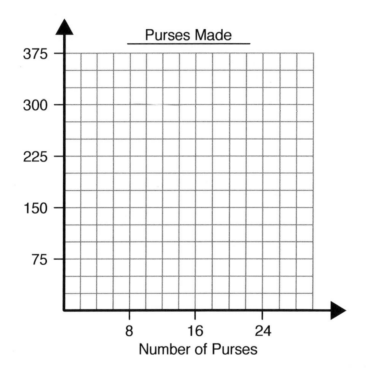

301. Write an equation for cost, C, as a function of purses produced, p.

302. How much would it cost to produce 21 purses?

303. A basketball team scored 64 points in their last game. The team scored 9 points at the free-throw line (worth 1 point each) and 3 three-point baskets. The rest of the points were scored on two-point baskets. Write an equation that can be solved to determine how many two-point baskets, t, the team scored.

305. Meghan and Walter paddled a canoe down a river with a current. The rate the canoe traveled in still water was x miles per hour and the current's average speed was c miles per hour. They traveled 5 miles downstream in 3.5 hours. Write an equation to represent this information.

$$3, 6, 12, 24, 48, \ldots$$

304. Find the ninth term in the above pattern.

306. Write the following verbal sentence as an equation: "Ten more than the quotient of a number, n, and 2 is 24."

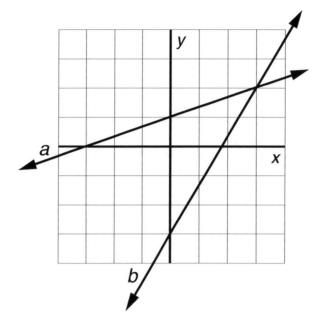

307. The two lines shown on the grid above pass through (3, 2). One line passes through the point (0, 1) and the other passes through the point (0, -3). Write a linear equation to identify each line.

308. Find the equation of the line with a slope of 7 containing the point (1, 8). Write your answer in slope-intercept form.

309. What is the slope of the line 8x + 4y +1 = 0?

310. Graph $y = x^2$ and $y = -x^2$.

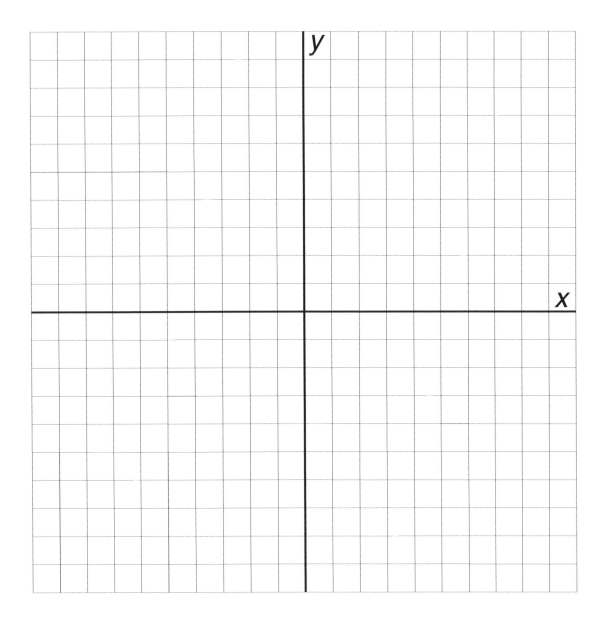

You plan to refinish the hardwood floors in your house so you call two companies to ask about renting a sander. The first company that you call charges $75.00 plus $25.00 per day to rent a sander. The second company charges $85.00 plus $20.00 per day to rent the sander.

311. On the grid below, sketch a graph that represents the total cost to rent the sander for both companies for the first five days. Be sure to label the axes.

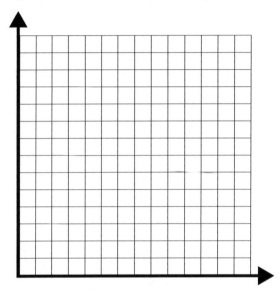

312. Write an equation for cost to rent the sander, C, as a function of days rented, d, for the first company that you called.

313. Write an equation for cost to rent the sander, C, as a function of days rented, d, for the second company that you called.

314. For how many days would the companies charge the SAME price?

315. If you work on the project only at night, you will need the sander for five days. Which company should you rent from? Explain your answer.

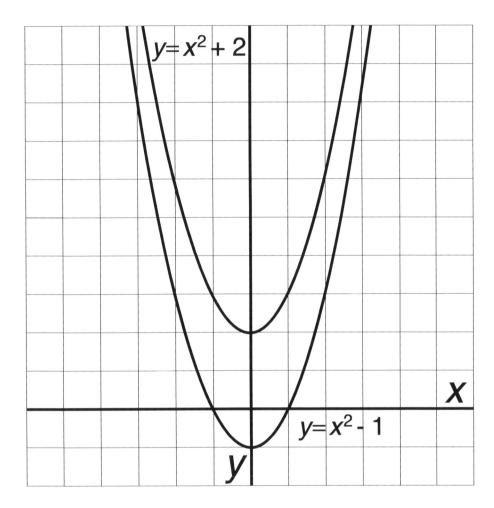

316. Changing the constant, c, in the equation $y = x^2 + c$ translates the graph of the parabola up or down. How does the graph of $y = x^2 + 2$ and $y = x^2 - 1$ compare to the graph of $y = x^2$?

317. Sketch a graph that illustrates the possible relationship between the number of hours spent studying for a test and the grade a student receives on the test. Be sure to label the axes.

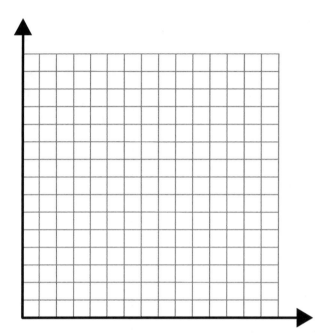

318. The vertex of a parabola is either the maximum or minimum value of the graph. The vertex is a maximum if the parabola is concave down and a minimum if the parabola is concave up. The x-coordinate of the vertex is the x-value of the maximum or minimum of the function, and the y-coordinate of the vertex is the maximum value of the function. If a quadratic function is in standard form, $y = ax^2 + bx + c$, the maximum or minimum value of the function is the y value when $x = -b/2a$. Find the minimum value of the function $f(x) = 4x + x^2$.

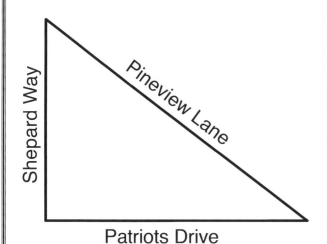

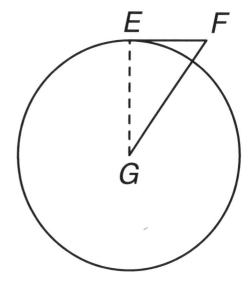

319. The map above shows two routes Kate can drive to school. If Shepard Way is six miles long and Patriots Drive is eight miles long, how many miles will she save by driving on Pineview Lane instead of on Shepard Way and Patriots Drive?

   a. 4.0 miles
   b. 7.7 miles
   c. 8.0 miles
   d. 14.0 miles

321. In figure above, $\overline{EF}$ is tangent to circle G at point E. $\overline{EF}$ = 8 cm and $\overline{GF}$ = 17 cm. What is the length of $\overline{EG}$?

   a. 8 cm
   b. 9 cm
   c. 15 cm
   d. 19 cm

320. A quadrilateral has sides measuring x, $2x$, $4x - 2$, and $3x + 6$. What is the length of its longest side if its perimeter is 64 cm?

   a. 6 cm
   b. 16 cm
   c. 22 cm
   d. 24 cm

322. If $\triangle ABC \cong \triangle DEF$, then which of the following is NOT a true statement?

   a. $\overline{AC} \cong \overline{DF}$
   b. $\angle B \cong \angle E$
   c. $\overline{FE} \cong \overline{BA}$
   d. $\angle F \cong \angle C$

323. Equilateral triangle, $\triangle ABC$, is inscribed in circle O. Each of the following statements is true EXCEPT

    a. The measure of minor arc AB equals the measure of minor arc BC.
    b. The measure of arc AB is 60°.
    c. $\overline{AB}$ and $\overline{AC}$ are equidistant from the O, the center of the circle.
    d. $\angle ABC = 60°$

325. A triangular prism has bases that are right triangles. Which of the following could be the shape of its lateral faces?

    a. trapezoids
    b. right triangles
    c. parallelograms
    d. isosceles triangles

324. An astronaut mathematically expressed the amount of space occupied by an asteroid. The astronaut reported the asteroid's _____.

    a. surface area
    b. circumference
    c. diameter
    d. volume

326. Which of the following cannot be the shape of a cross section of a right circular cone?

    a. an ellipse
    b. a rectangle
    c. a triangle
    d. a circle

327. If the ratio of the corresponding sides of similar polygons (or the radii of similar circles) is $m{:}n$, then the ratio of their areas is $m^2{:}n^2$. If the radius of a sphere is multiplied by a factor of 4 to create a larger sphere, what is the ratio of the surface areas of the two spheres?

    a. 1 to 64
    b. 1 to 16
    c. 1 to 8
    d. 1 to 4

328. How many cubic feet of brick are needed to build a square pyramid with a height of 100 feet and a base with a side length of 60 feet?

    a. 40,000 cubic feet
    b. 120,000 cubic feet
    c. 156,000 cubic feet
    d. 360,000 cubic feet

329. Twice the measure of the complement of a certain angle is equal to 20° less than the measure of the supplement of that angle. What is the measure of the angle?

    a. 20°
    b. 45°
    c. 70°
    d. 160°

330. What is the standard form of the equation of a circle with a radius of 2 units and center (9, -1)?

    a. $(x - 9)^2 + (y + 1)^2 = 2$
    b. $(x - 9)^2 + (y + 1)^2 = 2^2$
    c. $(x - 9)^2 + (y - 1)^2 = 2^2$
    d. $(x - 9)^2 + (y - 1)^2 = 2$

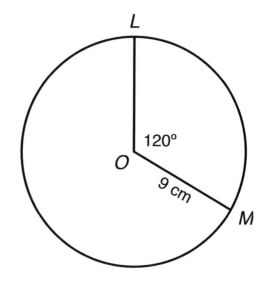

Plot A 12

?

Plot B 15

25

331. Jane is considering using two similar plots of land to garden as shown in the above diagram. One of the dimensions of the plot A is unreadable. If the dimensions are in feet, which of the following would be the area of Plot A?

a. 180 square feet
b. 240 square feet
c. 375 square feet
d. 586 square feet

333. What is the length of arc LM in the circle?

a. 3π cm
b. 6π cm
c. 9π cm
d. 18π cm

332. What is the approximate length of $\overline{AB}$ when the coordinates of its endpoints are $A(-8, 4)$ and $B(4, 9)$?

a. 6.4 units
b. 13.0 units
c. 13.9 units
d. 17.0 units

334. What is the measure of each exterior angle of a regular pentagon?

a. 60°
b. 72°
c. 108°
d. 360°

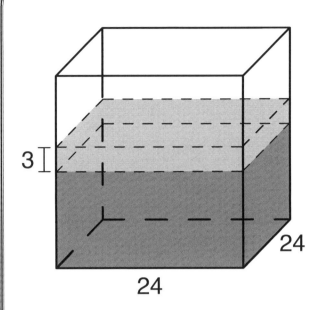

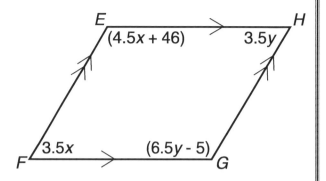

Use the figure shown above to solve the following problems.

336. Which of the following would be the value of x?

   a. 14.89
   b. 16.75
   c. 19.14
   d. 22.34

337. Which of the following would be the value of y?

   a. 16.82
   b. 18.50
   c. 20.56
   d. 61.67

335. The volume of an irregularly shaped solid can be found by dropping the solid into a container of liquid and measuring the rise of the water level. The change in the water's volume equals the volume of the solid and is called the solid's displacement. A rock is dropped in the square prism above causing the water level to rise three centimeters. What would be the volume of the rock?

   a. 3 cubic centimeters
   b. 72 cubic centimeters
   c. 576 cubic centimeters
   d. 1,728 cubic centimeters

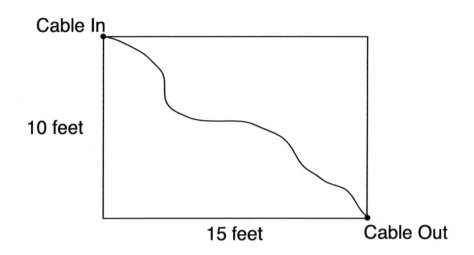

Cable In

10 feet

15 feet   Cable Out

338. Tina wants to run a cable wire from one room to the next. She will run the wire in her basement underneath the rooms. A diagram of the setup is shown above. ABOUT how many feet of wire will Tina need?

a. 15 feet
b. 17 feet
c. 18 feet
d. 24 feet

339. John's Pizza sells a pizza with a 12-inch diameter for $9.95. Dominic's Pizza sells a pizza with a 16-inch diameter for $14.95. How much of a better deal is the the larger pizza in terms of cost per square inch of pizza, rounded to the nearest whole number?

a. about $.014 per square inch
b. about $.057 per square inch
c. about $.062 per square inch
d. about $.093 per square inch

340. A floor tile company manufactures tiles in the shape of regular hexagons. Which of the following would be the measure of each interior angle?

a. 90°
b. 116°
c. 120°
d. 135°

1 cm

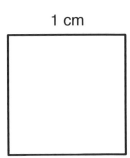

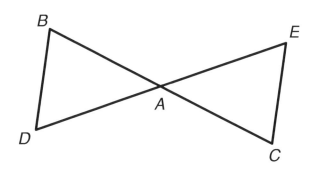

341. How many of the squares above can be arranged side-by-side without any gaps to create a similar figure with a perimeter of 20 cm?

    a. 5
    b. 20
    c. 25
    d. 30

343. If $\overline{EA} \cong \overline{DA}$ and $\overline{CA} \cong \overline{BA}$, then $\triangle EAC \cong \triangle DAB$ by which postulate?

    a. Side Side Side
    b. Angle Side Angle
    c. Side Angle Side
    d. Side Angle Angle

342. Each of the following statements is true EXCEPT

    a. Any two equilateral triangles are similar.
    b. Any two squares are similar.
    c. Any two isosceles triangles are similar.
    d. Any two regular pentagons are similar.

344. A diameter of a circle has endpoints $R(8, 1)$ and $C(-16, -6)$. What is the approximate length of the radius?

    a. 4.7 units
    b. 9.4 units
    c. 12.5 units
    d. 25 units

345. Which of the following statements is NOT true?

    a. Every cross section of a prism parallel to the bases is congruent to the bases.

    b. The net of the lateral surface of a right cylinder is a rectangle.

    c. Every cross section of a pyramid parallel to the base is congruent to the base.

    d. All cross sections of a sphere passing through the sphere's center are congruent.

347. Two parallel lines with the equations $y = x + 1$ and $y = mx + 9$ contain opposite sides of a square. What is the value of m in the second equation?

    a. -2
    b. -1/2
    c. 1
    d. 2

346. The length, width, and height of a cube are changed to double their original size. By what factor does the surface area of the cube increase?

    a. 2
    b. 4
    c. 6
    d. 8

348. $\overline{PQ}$ is the diameter of circle O. If the endpoints of the diameter are (2, 14) and (18, 6), what are the coordinates of the center of circle O?

    a. (-8, -10)
    b. (10, 10)
    c. (-10, -4)
    d. (-8, -4)

Erica's room is shaped as in the figure below.

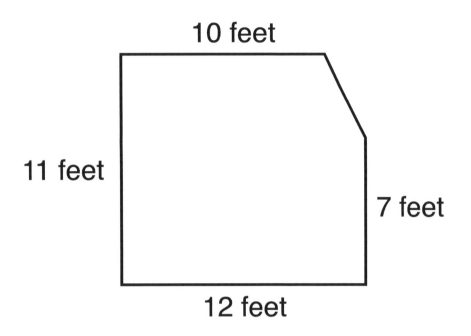

10 feet

11 feet

7 feet

12 feet

349. She wants to put up a wallpaper border that comes in rolls of 15 linear feet around her entire room. How many rolls should she buy?

    a. 2
    b. 3
    c. 4
    d. 5

350. Erica also wants to put new carpet in the room. How much carpet does she need? Round your answer to the nearest square foot.

    a. 90 square feet
    b. 110 square feet
    c. 118 square feet
    d. 128 square feet

113

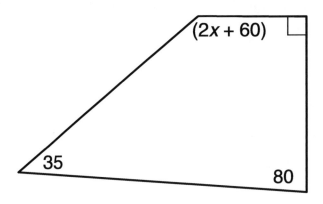

351. What is the value of x in the figure shown above?

    a. 15
    b. 42.5
    c. 47.5
    d. 65

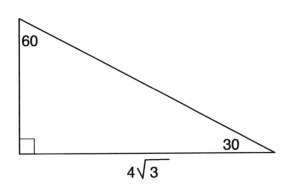

352. In the triangle shown above, which of the following would be the length of the hypotenuse?

    a. 4
    b. 6
    c. 7
    d. 8

353. A polygon is a closed figure in a plane made up of line segments connected endpoint to endpoint. Each line segment is called a side, each endpoint is called a vertex, and a diagonal is a line segment that connects two non-consecutive vertices. An octagon is an eight-sided polygon. How many diagonals can be drawn from one vertex of an octagon?

    a. 5
    b. 9
    c. 10
    d. 20

114

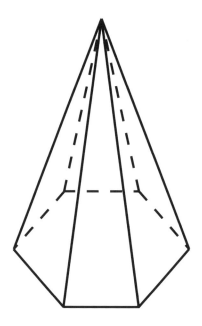

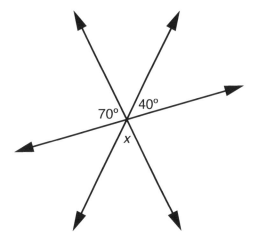

354. What is another name for the hexagonal pyramid shown above?

   a. hexahedron
   b. heptahedron
   c. hexagonal prism
   d. octahedron

356. What is the measure of angle x in the above diagram?

   a. 11.25°
   b. 16°
   c. 32°
   d. 70°

355. $\triangle ABC$ is similar to $\triangle DEF$. Which of the following statements is NOT true?

   a. $\angle E = \angle B$
   b. $\dfrac{AB}{DE} = \dfrac{BC}{EF}$
   c. $\dfrac{AC}{DF} = \dfrac{AB}{EF}$
   d. $\angle C = \angle F$

357. A triangle with an *exterior* altitude could be which of the following?

   a. obtuse
   b. right
   c. acute
   d. equiangular

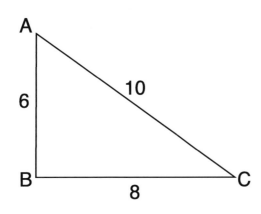

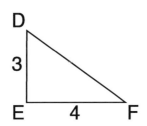

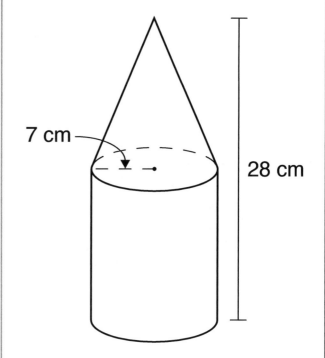

7 cm

28 cm

ΔABC is similar to ΔDEF. Use the above figure below to solve the following problems.

358. Which of the following would be the scale factor of ΔABC to ΔDEF?

    a. .5
    b. .75
    c. 2
    d. 5

359. What is the ratio of the area of ΔABC to the area of ΔDEF?

    a. 2:1
    b. 4:1
    c. 6:1
    d. 10:1

360. A right cone and a right cylinder have been placed with the cone's base touching one of the cylinder's bases to create the above figure. The radius of both the cone and the cylinder is 7 centimeters, both have the same height, and the total height of the figure is 28 centimeters. What is the volume of the figure? (Let π = 3.14.)

    a. 2,872.053 cm^3
    b. 718.013 cm^3
    c. 2,154.04 cm^3
    d. 1,436.027 cm^3

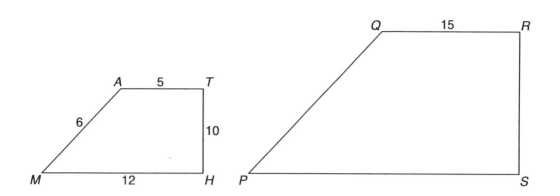

PQRS is similar to *MATH*. Use the figures shown above to solve the following problems.

361. Which of the following is the scale factor of *MATH* to *PQRS*?

    a. 2
    b. 3
    c. 6
    d. 10

362. What is the length of *PS*?

    a. 14
    b. 16
    c. 24
    d. 36

363. What is the ratio of the perimeter of *MATH* to *PQRS*?

    a. 1:1.5
    b. 1:2
    c. 1:2.5
    d. 1:3

364. At a distance of 35 feet from a flagpole, the angle of elevation from the ground to the top of the flagpole is 30°. What is the height of the flagpole?

    a. 20.2 feet
    b. 35.0 feet
    c. 60.6 feet
    d. 70.0 feet

366. A television stand in the shape of a cube measures three feet on each edge. If the stand weighs 2.5 pounds per cubic foot, what is the total weight, in pounds, of the stand?

    a. 10. 8 pounds
    b. 22.5 pounds
    c. 27 pounds
    d. 67.5 pounds

365. In isosceles triangle *NEW*, the interior angle *E* measures 110°. Which of the following are the degree measures of all three interior angles of the triangle°

    a. 110°, 110°, and 140°
    b. 110°, 70°, and 70°
    c. 110°, 110°, and 110°
    d. 35°, 35°, and 110°

367. What is the perimeter of an isosceles right triangle whose hypotenuse is $4\sqrt{2}$ cm?

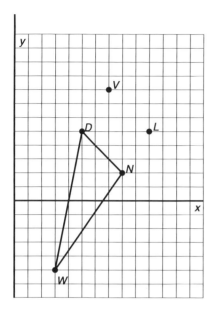

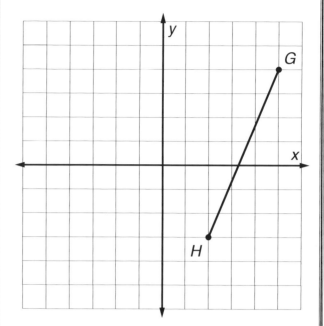

368. Val wants to draw $\triangle LVE$ on the above grid so that it is congruent to $\triangle WDN$, which has verticies at (3, -5), (5, 5), and (8, 2). She located point V at (7, 8) and point L at (10, 5). Which of the following are possible coordinates of point E?

    a. (5, -2)
    b. (3, -4)
    c. (11, 16)
    d. (12, 15)

369. All of the following postulates prove triangles are congruent EXCEPT

    a. Side Side Side
    b. Angle Angle Angle
    c. Side Angle Side
    d. Angle Side Angle

370. What is the approximate length of $\overline{GH}$ in the graph above?

    a. 6.7 units
    b. 7.6 units
    c. 10 units
    d. 58 units

371. The surface area of a cube is 294 cm². What is the length of its edges?

    a. 6.6 cm
    b. 7 cm
    c. 8.6 cm
    d. 24.5 cm

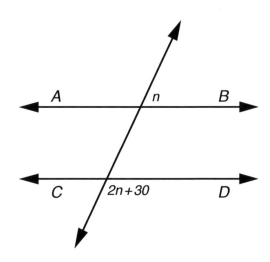

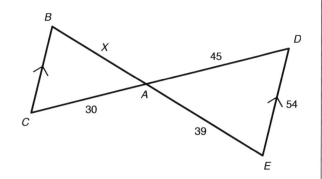

372. If $\overline{AB} \parallel \overline{CD}$, what is the value of n as shown in the above diagram?

    a. 20°
    b. 30°
    c. 50°
    d. 70°

374. What is the length of $\overline{AB}$ in the above diagram?

    a. 24.0 units
    b. 26.0 units
    c. 34.6 units
    d. 36.0 units

373. Each of the following statements is true EXCEPT

    a. Vertical angles could be complementary.
    b. The angles of a linear pair are always supplementary.
    c. If angle A = 60°, and angle B = 120°, then the angles are supplementary.
    d. Vertical angles are adjacent angles.

375. The graph of which of the following functions is NOT congruent to the graph of $y = 3x^2 + 6$?

    a. $y = 3x^2 - 6$
    b. $y = -3x^2 - 6$
    c. $y = x^2 + 6$
    d. $y = -3x^2 + 6$

376. *PS* and *IR* intersect at a point *A* so that *A* is halfway between *P* and *S* and also halfway between *I* and *R*. Which of the following statements must be TRUE?

    a. $\angle PAR$ and $\angle SAI$ are supplementary.
    b. $\angle PAR$ and $\angle SAI$ are complementary.
    c. $\overline{PS} \perp \overline{IR}$
    d. $\angle PAI = \angle RAS$

378. A sculpture has a volume of 112 cubic feet and a height of 8 feet. A similar sculpture is 2 feet tall. What is the volume of the smaller sculpture?

    a. 1.75 cubic feet
    b. 7 cubic feet
    c. 9.33 cubic feet
    d. 28 cubic feet

377. The surface area of a sphere is found using the formula $S = 4\pi r^2$. Which of the following represents the surface area of a sphere with a radius of $3m^3np^2$?

    a. $24\pi m^3 np^2$
    b. $12\pi m^3 np^4$
    c. $144\pi m^5 n^2 p^4$
    d. $36\pi m^6 n^2 p^4$

379. If $y = 5x^2$, $y = 1/5x^2$, $y = -5x^2$ are graphed on the same coordinate plane, which two graphs will be congruent?

    a. $y = 5x^2$ and $y = 1/5x^2$
    b. $y = 5x^2$ and $y = -5x^2$
    c. $y = 1/5x^2$ and $y = -5x^2$
    d. none of the graphs

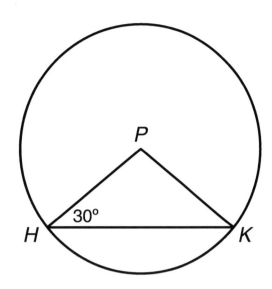

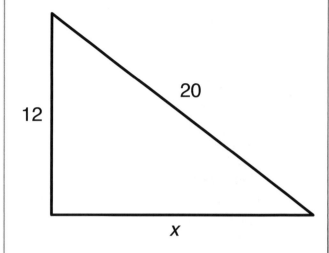

380. Point *P* is the center of the circle above. If ∠*PHK* = 30°, what is the measure of arc *HK*?

    a. 30°
    b. 60°
    c. 120°
    d. 240°

382. What is the length of side *x* in the above triangle?

    a. 8.0 feet
    b. 16.0 feet
    c. 23.3 feet
    d. 32.0 feet

381. If the measure of each interior angle of a regular polygon is 100° more than its adjacent exterior angle, what type of polygon is it?

    a. hexagon
    b. octagon
    c. nonagon
    d. decagon

383. *M* is the midpoint of $\overline{XY}$. What are the coordinates of *Y* if *X* has coordinates (-11, -6) and *M* has coordinates (1, -2.5)?

    a. (-5, -4.25)
    b. (-6, -1.75)
    c. (13, 1)
    d. (10, 0)

384. Which of the following statements is NOT true?

    a. Any interior and exterior angle of a regular polygon are supplementary.
    b. There is a polygon whose interior angles add up to 1,000°.
    c. There is a polygon whose interior angles add up to 1,260°.
    d. The larger the number of sides of a polygon, the greater the sum of its interior angles.

385. Each of the following statements is true EXCEPT

    a. Concentric circles share the same center.
    b. If two circles are congruent, then their diameters are congruent.
    c. A chord of a circle could also be a diameter.
    d. A line tangent to a circle intersects the circle in exactly two points.

386. Walter uses a rectangular box to store his family photos and mementos. The dimensions of the box are 18 inches by 12 inches by 10.5 inches. What is the volume of the box?

    a. 756 cubic inches
    b. 1,062 cubic inches
    c. 2,160 cubic inches
    d. 2,268 cubic inches

387. What is the length of the diagonal of a rectangle whose width is 5 cm and whose length is 12 cm?

    a. 7 cm
    b. 10.9 cm
    c. 13 cm
    d. 17 cm

388. A 15-foot ladder leans against the side of a building creating an angle of 37° with the building. Which equation can be used to find the distance, d, of the base of the ladder from the side of the building?

    a. $\sin 37° = 15/d$
    b. $\cos 37° = d/15$
    c. $\tan 37° = d/15$
    d. $\sin 37° = d/15$

389. Which equation represents the relationship between the surface area of a sphere, S, and the volume of a sphere, V?

    a. $S/V = 3/r$
    b. $S/V = 3$
    c. $S/V = 1/3r$
    d. $S/V = 12/r$

390. What is the minimum amount of cardboard needed to make a box that is 18 cm long, 15 cm wide, and 10 cm tall?

    a. 600 cm^2
    b. 660 cm^2
    c. $1{,}200 \text{ cm}^2$
    d. $2{,}700 \text{ cm}^2$

391. A cylinder with a height of 5 feet has a total surface area of 18π square feet. Which of the following would be the radius of this cylinder?

    a. 10 feet
    b. 6 feet
    c. 2 feet
    d. 8 feet

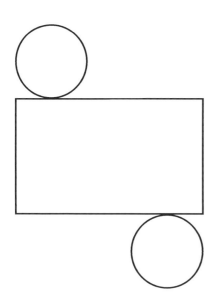

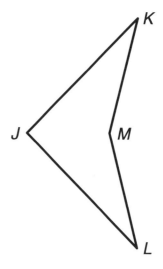

392. What 3-dimensional figure does the above net represent?

    a. a cylinder
    b. a cone
    c. a sphere
    d. a rectangular prism

394. What is the sum of the measures of the interior angles of convex polygon *JKLM*?

    a. 180°
    b. 360°
    c. 540°
    d. 720°

393. Each of the following statements is true EXCEPT

    a. The complement of an acute angle is acute.
    b. Bisecting an obtuse angle results in two right angles.
    c. The supplement of an acute angle is obtuse.
    d. The supplement of a right angle is a right angle.

395. What is the midpoint of $\overline{MN}$ with endpoints *M*(13, 3) and *N*(-7, -11)?

    a. (3, -4)
    b. (10, 7)
    c. (3, -7)
    d. (10, -4)

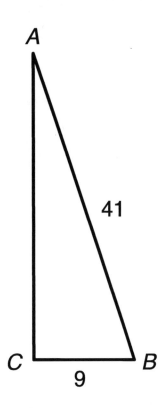

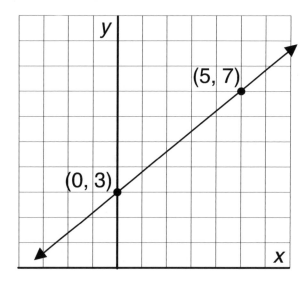

398. What is the slope of a line perpendicular to the line shown in the above diagram.

    a. 4/5
    b. -4/5
    c. 5/4
    d. -5/4

396. What is the length of $\overline{AC}$ as shown in the above diagram?

    a. 16
    b. 32
    c. 36
    d. 40

397. Given an equilateral triangle whose altitude has a length of 8 units, which of the following would be the approximate length of each side of the triangle?

    a. 6.18 units
    b. 9.24 units
    c. 10.76 units
    d. 14.30 units

399. One leg of a 45°-45°-90° triangle is 8 cm long. What is the length of its hypotenuse, rounded to the nearest hundredth?

    a. 5.66 cm
    b. 8.00 cm
    c. 11.31 cm
    d. 15.45 cm

Use the drawing to answer the questions below.

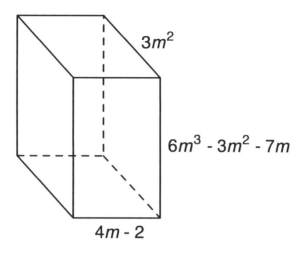

$3m^2$

$6m^3 - 3m^2 - 7m$

$4m - 2$

400. What is the volume of the solid?

    a. $72m^6 - 36m^5 - 120m^4 + 18m^3 + 42m^2$
    b. $72m^6 - 72m^5 - 66m^4 + 42m^3$
    c. $18m^5 - 9m^4 - 21m^3$
    d. $12m^3 - 6m^2$

401. What is the surface area?

    a. $18m^5 + 15m^4 - 33m^3 - 28m^2 + 14m$
    b. $18m^5 + 15m^4 - 45m^3 - 22m^2 + 14m$
    c. $36m^5 + 30m^4 - 114m^3 - 56m^2 + 28m$
    d. $36m^5 + 30m^4 - 66m^3 - 56m^2 + 28m$

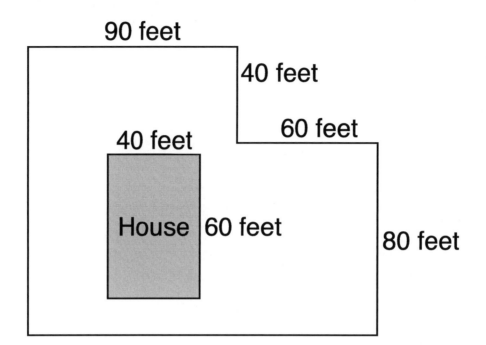

402. John is going to fertilize his lawn so he needs to know the area of his yard. The above diagram gives the dimensions of the lawn and those of his house. What is the area of the lawn in square feet?

    a. 6,000 square feet
    b. 8,400 square feet
    c. 13,200 square feet
    d. 15,600 square feet

403. Which of the following equations describes a line that passes through the point (6, 3) with a slope of 3/2?

    a. $y = 1.5x - 6$
    b. $y = 1.5x - 1$
    c. $3y = 2x - 3$
    d. $y = -1.5x + 12$

404. Which of the following is the diameter of a circle whose circumference is 56π inches?

    a. 18 inches
    b. 28 inches
    c. 56 inches
    d. 112 inches

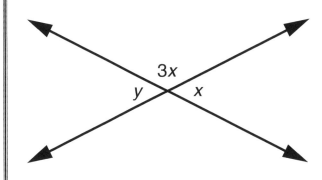

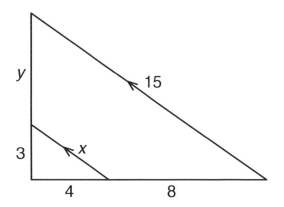

405. What is the value of *y* in the diagram above?

    a. 36°
    b. 45°
    c. 108°
    d. 135°

406. A polygon is a closed figure in a plane made up of line segments connected endpoint to endpoint. Each line segment is called a side, each endpoint is called a vertex, and a diagonal is a line segment that connects two non-consecutive vertices. A hexagon is a six-sided polygon. How many total diagonals can be drawn in a hexagon?

    a. 9
    b. 12
    c. 15
    d. 18

Use the figure shown above to solve the following problems.

407. What is the value of *y*?

    a. 3
    b. 4
    c. 6
    d. 8

408. What is the value of *x*?

    a. 5
    b. 6
    c. 7.5
    d. 10

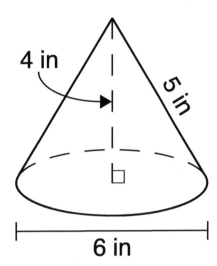

4 in

5 in

6 in

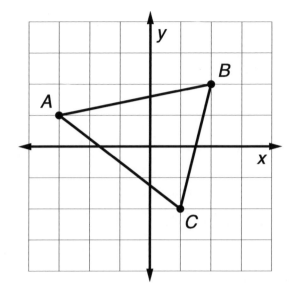

409. The equation describing the volume of a cone is $V = (1/3)\pi r^2 h$, where r is the radius of the circular surface and h is the height of the cone. What is the volume of the cone above?

   a. 9π in^3
   b. 12π in^3
   c. 18π in^3
   d. 36π in^3

411. What is the perimeter of $\triangle ABC$ in the graph above, rounded to nearest whole number?

   a. 13
   b. 14
   c. 15
   d. 16

410. A ball is immersed in a container of water and displaces 972π cubic centimeters of water. What is the radius of the ball?

   a. 9 centimeters
   b. 11 centimeters
   c. 14 centimeters
   d. 17 centimeters

412. The degree total of the interior angles of polygon is 1,260. How many sides does this polygon have?

   a. 5
   b. 6
   c. 7
   d. 9

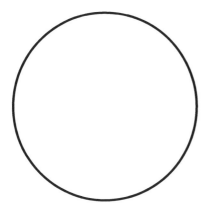

circumference = 100 feet

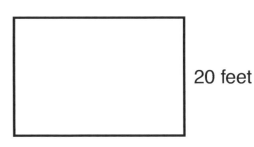

20 feet

30 feet

413. A landscaper has 100 bricks that are each one foot long. He is planting shrubs surrounded by mulch and trying to decide between a circular shape and a rectangular shape. The above diagrams show the area set aside for the trees. How many square feet greater is the area of the circle compared to the rectangle, rounded to nearest whole number?

   a. 42 ft^2
   b. 196 ft^2
   c. 202 ft^2
   d. 345 ft^2

414. If the ratio of the corresponding edges (or heights or radii) of similar solids is $m{:}n$, then the ratio of their volumes is $m^3{:}n^3$. The radii of the bases of two similar right cylinders are 4 inches and 10 inches respectively. What is the ratio of their volumes?

   a. 400:1,000
   b. 64:1,000
   c. 16:100
   d. 4:10

415. What is the measure of an exterior angle of a regular heptagon?

   a. 128.57°
   b. 102.86°
   c. 77.14°
   d. 51.43°

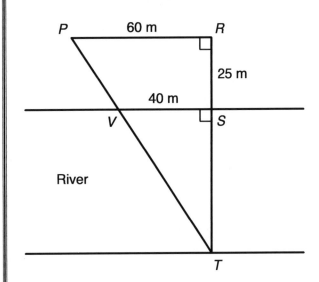

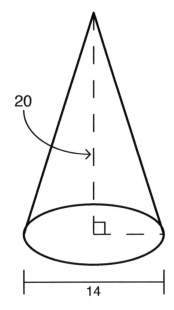

416. A park ranger estimates the distance across the river, $\overline{ST}$, by sighting a tree on the opposite bank. He draws triangles using known distances as shown so that $\angle TSV = \angle TRP$. What is the distance across the river?

a. 25 meters
b. 50 meters
c. 75 meters
d. 100 meters

418. The height of the cone shown below is increased by scale factor of 5. By what factor is the volume of the new cone greater than that of the original cone?

a. 5
b. 10
c. 15
d. 25

417. The hypotenuse of a 30°-60°-90° triangle is 12 inches. What is the length of its longer leg, rounded to the nearest hundredth?

a. 6.00 inches
b. 9.59 inches
c. 10.39 inches
d. 11.54 inches

419. The ratio of the angles in a triangle is 2 to 6 to 7. What is the measure of the largest angle?

a. 12°
b. 24°
c. 72°
d. 84°

132

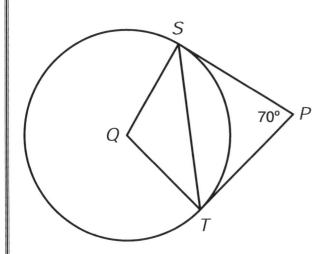

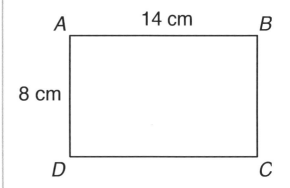

420. $\overline{SP}$ and $\overline{TP}$ are tangent segments to circle Q. The measure of $\angle P$ is 70°. What is the measure of $\angle QTS$?

   a. 70°
   b. 100°
   c. 110°
   d. 35°

422. What is the volume of the solid created by rotating rectangle ABCD 360° about side AD?

   a. 224π cm^3
   b. 392π cm^3
   c. 896π cm^3
   d. $1,568\pi$ cm^3

421. A train travels 15 miles north from point X and then turns and travels 15 miles due west to reach point Y. If instead it had traveled the direct path from point X to point Y, how many miles would the train have traveled, rounded to the nearest whole number?

   a. 15 miles
   b. 21 miles
   c. 25 miles
   d. 30 miles

423. Given a square whose perimeter is 72, what is the length of the diagonal, rounded to the nearest tenth?

   a. 9.0
   b. 25.5
   c. 50.9
   d. 101.8

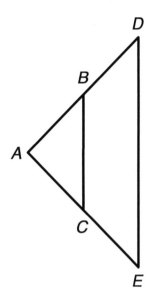

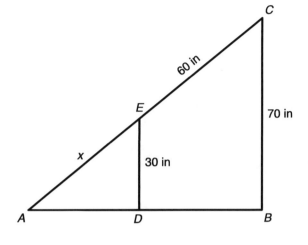

424. Triangle *ABC* is isosceles, therefore line segment *AB* = line segment *AC*. If the angle BAC measures 70° and line segment DE is parallel to line segment BC, what is the measure of angle DBC?

a. 55°
b. 125°
c. 135°
d. 141°

426. In the figure above, $\overline{BC}$ = 70 in, $\overline{CE}$ = 60 in, and $\overline{DE}$ = 30 in. What is the length of $\overline{AE}$ in the figure above?

a. 25 in
b. 35 in
c. 45 in
d. 55 in

425. The length of a rectangle is three times its width. The perimeter is 64 units. What is the length of the diagonal of the rectangle, rounded to the nearest whole number?

a. 24
b. 25
c. 27
d. 32

427. The wheels on a mountain bike have a 15-inch radius. What is the circumference of one of the wheels?

a. 15π
b. 30π
c. 60π
d. 225π

Cammie got a new puppy for her birthday. She and her father are going to build a dog house. Below is a scale drawing of the dog house.

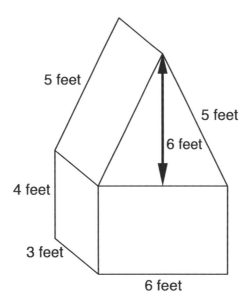

428. What is the area of the roof of the doghouse?

    a. 15 ft^2
    b. 36 ft^2
    c. 42 ft^2
    d. 66 ft^2

429. Plywood comes in sheets that are six feet-by-four feet. Not including the roof, how many sheets of plywood will they need to construct the house?

    a. 1
    b. 2
    c. 3
    d. 4

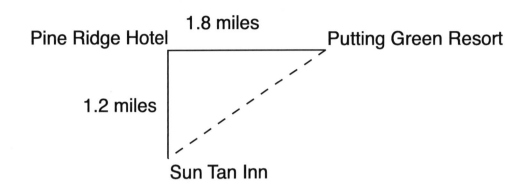

Pine Ridge Hotel — 1.8 miles — Putting Green Resort

1.2 miles

Sun Tan Inn

430. Pine Ridge Hotel is 1.8 miles from Putting Green Resort. The Sun Tan Inn is 1.2 miles south of Pine Ridge. A hotel chain buys all three hotels and the project manager proposes building a shortcut path to directly connect the Sun Tan Inn and Putting Green Resort. To the nearest tenth of a mile, what is the length of this new path?

a. 2.2 miles
b. 2.4 miles
c. 2.6 miles
d. 3.0 miles

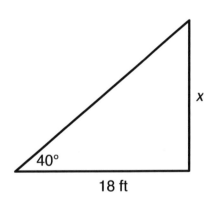

40°

18 ft

x

431. What is the value of x in the right triangle above? (Round your answer to the nearest tenth.)

a. 12.6 feet
b. 15.1 feet
c. 16.4 feet
d. 17.9 feet

The midpoint of a segment with endpoints (x_1, y_1) and (x_2, y_2) is:

$$\left(\frac{x_1 + x_2}{2} , \frac{y_1 + y_2}{2} \right)$$

432. M is the midpoint of $\overline{XY}$. What are the coordinates of Y if X has coordinates $(1, 10)$ and M has coordinates $(-5, 3)$?

a. (10, -3)
b. (-2, 6.5)
c. (-10, 6)
d. (-11, -4)

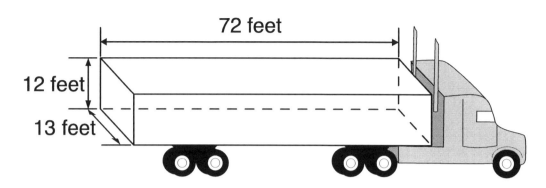

433. How many cubic feet of merchandise can fit into the tractor trailer shown above?

    a. 2,040 ft^3

    b. 3,912 ft^3

    c. 11,232 ft^3

    d. 12,168 ft^3

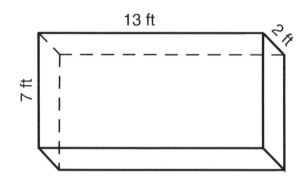

434. The figure above shows the dimension of a box. If all of the dimensions are increased by 3 feet, what will be the total surface area of the new box?

    a. 245 ft^2

    b. 290 ft^2

    c. 580 ft^2

    d. 800 ft^2

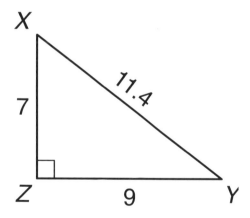

435. What is the volume of the solid created by rotating triangle XYZ 360° about side YZ?

    a. 44π cubic units

    b. 147π cubic units

    c. 189π cubic units

    d. 308π cubic units

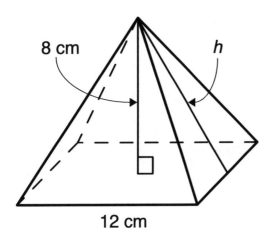

8 cm   h

12 cm

436. What is the surface area of the right square pyramid shown above?

a. 144 cm^2
b. 240 cm^2
c. 324 cm^2
d. 384 cm^2

437. The distance formula can be applied to writing the equation of a circle. A circle, by definition, is the set of all points in a plane at a given distance from given point. The given distance is the radius and the given point is the center of the circle. A diameter of a circle has endpoints $C(-6, 7)$ and $J(-2, 12)$. Which of the following would be the approximate radius of the circle?

a. 5.8
b. 2.9
c. 3.2
d. 4.1

Coplanar lines $\overline{UV}$, $\overline{WX}$, and $\overline{YZ}$ intersect at a point T as shown in the diagram below.

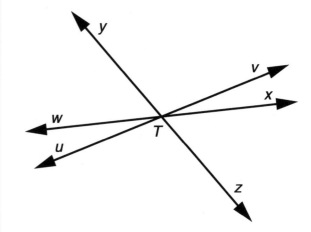

438. If the measure of ∠WTZ is 140° and the measure of ∠YTV is 105°, what is the measure of ∠VTX?

a. 35°
b. 40°
c. 55°
d. 60°

439. What is the measure of UTY?

a. 40°
b. 55°
c. 60°
d. 75°

Determine the value of x in each of the figures shown below.

440.

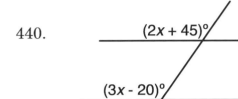

441.

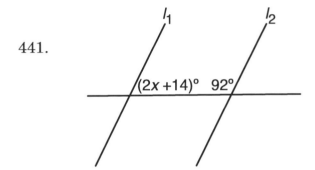

442.

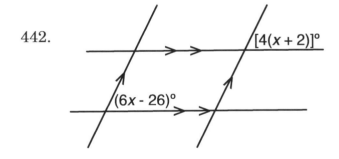

443.

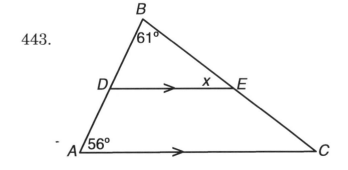

139

13 ft

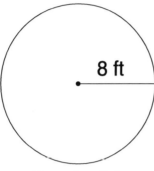

20 ft

8 ft

Depth: 8 ft   Depth: 6 ft

444. Your summer job involves cleaning people's pools. Neighbors A and B both want you to clean their pools, but you only have time to clean one pool. The pay is the same: $150.00 to clean a pool. Which one should you choose to clean? Let π = 3.14, and when solving this problem, be sure to show all your work.

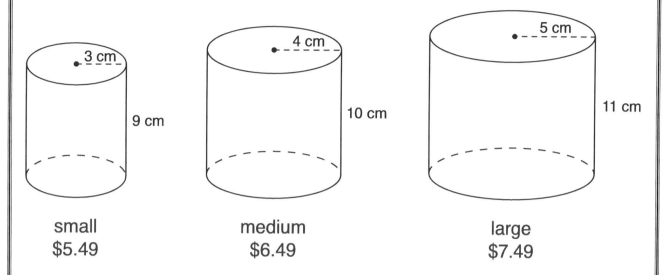

small
$5.49

medium
$6.49

large
$7.49

445. The concession stand at a concert hall sells popcorn in cylindrical shaped
     containers with dimensions as shown in the above diagram. Concert-goers can
     buy small, medium and large-sized popcorn. Which size is the best deal in
     terms of cost per cubic centimeter? Let $\pi = 3.14$, and when solving this
     problem, be sure to show all your work.

446. The perimeter of a rectangle is
     60 feet. The ratio of the width to
     the length is three to seven. What
     is the area of this rectangle?

447. Write an equation for the line that
     passes through the points (2, -2)
     and (-1, 7).

Find the area and perimeter (or circumference) of each figure shown below. Make sure to show all your work.

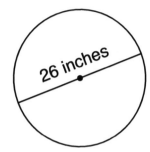

448.   circumference =

area =

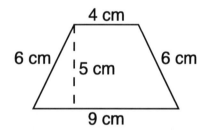

449.   perimeter =

area =

450.   perimeter =

area =

451.   perimeter =

area =

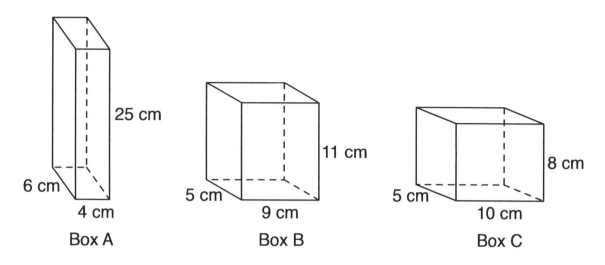

25 cm

6 cm

4 cm

Box A

11 cm

5 cm

9 cm

Box B

8 cm

5 cm

10 cm

Box C

452. A juice box company is developing a new line of super sized juice boxes. The marketing company is trying to pick a size for the box. They plan to put 450 milliliters of juice in a box. The box must be large enough to hold the juice but not so large that it does not appear to be full. Which of the boxes shown above would be the best choice for the new juice box design?

453. The midpoint of a segment with endpoints (x_1, y_1) and (x_2, y_2) is:

$$\left(\frac{x_1 + x_2}{2}, \frac{y_1 + y_2}{2} \right)$$

Find the midpoint of $\overline{AB}$ with endpoints $A(9, 6)$ and $B(-3, -4)$.

454. A stone company manufactures patio stones in the shape of regular octagons. What is the degree measure of each interior angle of the octagon?

Determine whether a quadrilateral with the given vertices is a parallelogram, rectangle, rhombus or square. Show your work and explain your answer.

455. M (0, 6), A (4, 11), T (5, 8), H (1, 3)

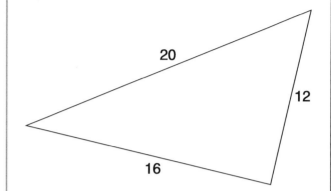

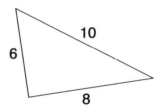

456. P (6, 2), Q (1, 1), R (-2, -3), S (3, -2)

457. Determine whether the triangles shown above are similar. Show all your work and explain how you arrived at your answer.

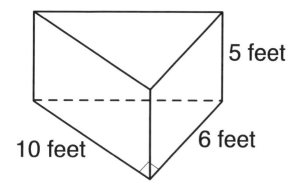

458. The base of a statue is shaped liked a prism as shown in the above diagram. The base is made entirely of cement. Determine the amount of cement used to make the base in cubic feet.

459. Michelle was kayaking due east at a steady speed of 8 miles per hour. As she paddled, the wind blew due south at 4 miles per hour causing her to change direction. What is the velocity of her kayak in miles per hour? Round your answer to the nearest tenth.

460. A television is advertised by giving the approximate length of the diagonal of its screen. A 72-inch television screen measures approximately 40 inches high. How wide is the television? Round your answer to the nearest inch.

Find the volume and surface area of each figure shown below.

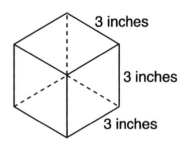

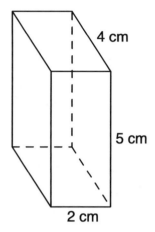

461.   volume =

        surface area =

463.   volume =

        surface area =

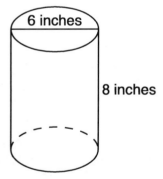

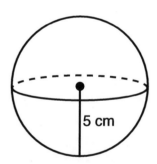

462.   volume =

        surface area =

464.   volume =

        surface area =

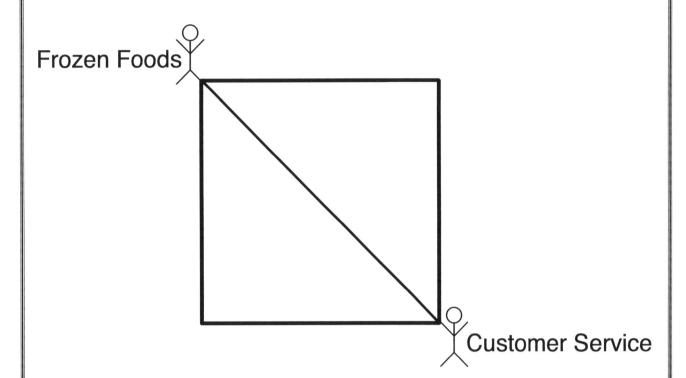

465. A grocery store has a square floor with an area of 60,025 square feet. All employees who work on the floor are required to wear headsets and wireless microphones. The range of the wireless system is 375 feet. In the diagram above, one employee is in the frozen foods section and the other is at the customer service desk. If the person in the frozen foods section has a question for the employee in customer service, can he ask it using the wireless microphone and headset? When solving this problem, be sure to show all your work.

466. The distance formula can be applied to writing the equation of a circle. A circle, by definition, is the set of all points in a plane at a given distance from given point. The given distance is the radius and the given point is the center of the circle. Write the equation of a circle with a radius of 4 units and center (3, 2).

468. A computer monitor measures approximately 11 inches high and 18 inches. wide. A monitor's size is advertised by giving the approximate length of the diagonal of its screen. How should this monitor be advertised? Round your answer to the nearest whole number.

467. What is the perimeter of a regular pentagon whose sides each measure 14 centimeters?

469. What is the perimeter of a square whose sides each measure 2.5 inches?

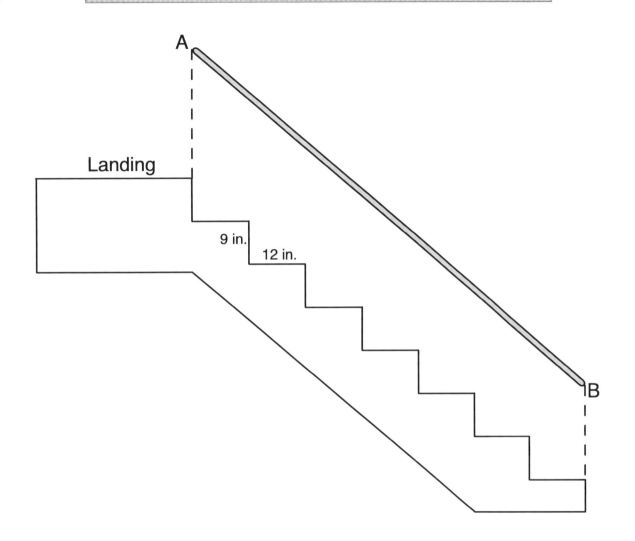

470. Walter plans to add a railing to the flight of stairs as shown in the above diagram. Based on this diagram, how long should this railing be? When solving this problem, be sure to show all your work.

The diagram below shows a race car track. The length of the straight-away section is 400 yards. The other ends are semicircles with a diameter of 100 yards.

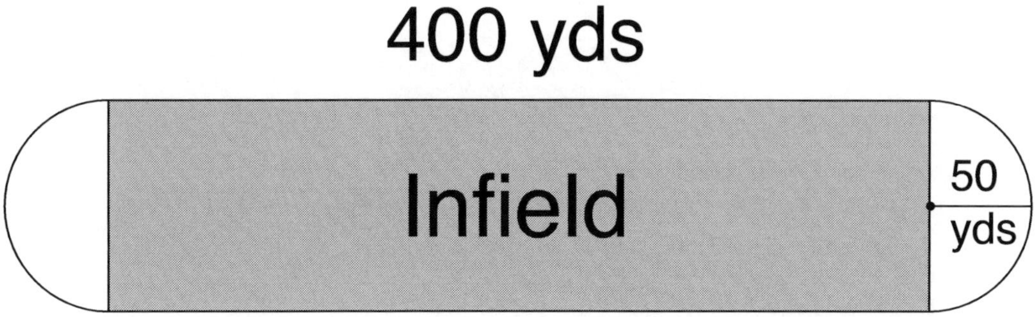

400 yds

Infield

50 yds

471. Find the total length of the track.

472. Find the area of the infield of the oval track.

150

Use the drawing to answer the questions below.

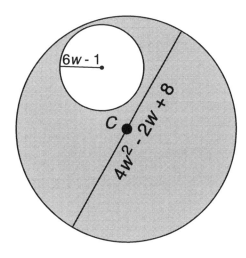

473. Identify the radius of the large circle.

474. Find the circumference of the small circle.

475. Find the area of the shaded region.

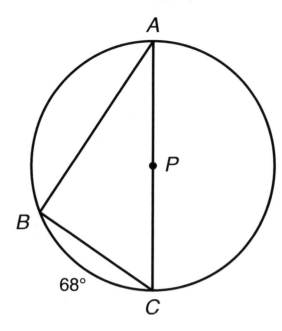

476. The clock above indicates a time of 4:00. Determine the measure of the angle made by the two hands on the clock. When solving this problem, be sure to show all your work.

478. Triangle *ABC* is inscribed in circle *P*. What is the measure of ∠*BCA*?

477. The distance formula can be used to find the perimeter of a figure graphed in an *x-y*-coordinate plane. Find the perimeter of ΔABC given its vertices are A(2, 1), B(-1, 5), and C(-7, -3).

479. The ratio of the measures of the angles of triangle ABC is 4 to 7 to 9. Identify the longest side. Show your work or explain your reasoning.

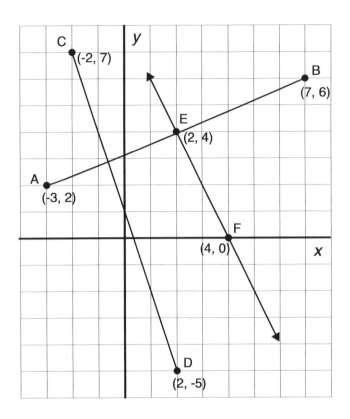

Use the graph shown above to solve the following problems.

480. Determine the slope of line segment AB.

481. Determine the distance between point C and point D.

482. Determine the midpoint of line segment EF.

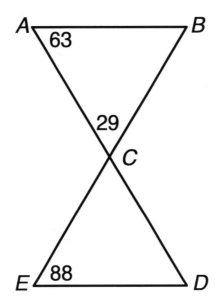

Use the figure shown above to solve the following problems.

483. Determine the measure of angle *CDE*.

484. Is *AB* parallel to *ED*? Show all of your work and explain your reasoning.

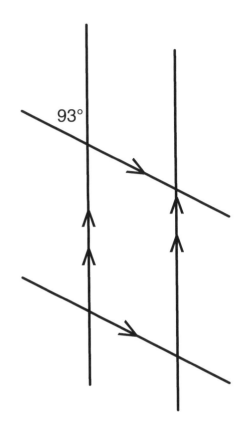

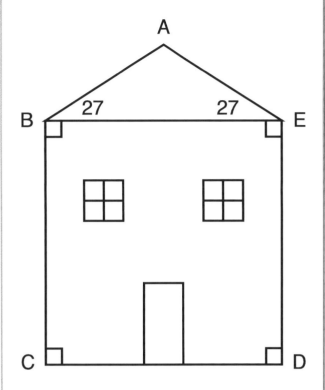

485. Fill in all the missing angles in the figure shown above.

486. What is the measure of angle A in the above diagram?

Use the drawing to answer the questions below.

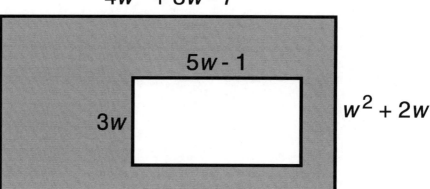

$$4w^2 + 3w - 7$$

$$5w - 1$$

$$3w$$

$$w^2 + 2w$$

487. Find the perimeter of the large rectangle.

488. Find the area of the shaded region.

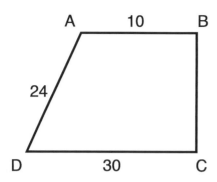
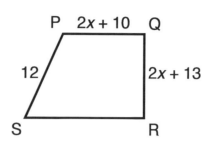

489. Polygon ABCD is similar to polygon PQRS. Determine the value of x and the length of side BC and SR. When solving this problem, be sure to show all your work.

490. The sum of the measures of the interior angles of a polygon can be expressed as $180(n - 2)°$, where n is the number of sides. Find the measure of each interior angle in a regular dodecagon, a twelve-sided polygon.

491. The radius of a circle is 12 cm more than the radius of a smaller circle. If the ratio of the two circles' circumferences is 4:1, what is the circumference of the larger circle?

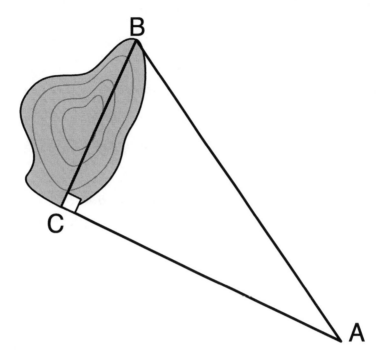

492. Heather wants to find the length of a pond (the distance between points B and C) but cannot measure it directly. Instead she sets a stake at a point A so that angle C is a right angle. By measuring, Heather found AB to be 140 feet and AC to be 98 feet. How far is it between B and C? Round your answer to the nearest whole number.

493. Given an isosceles right triangle whose hypotenuse has a length of 15, what are the lengths of the other two sides?

495. Find the circumference, in terms of pi, of a circle whose radius is seven centimeters.

494. The gate to the fence around the swimming pool at your house is in need of repair. The easiest thing to do is to reinforce it with a diagonal brace. If the length of the gate is six feet and the width is four feet and six inches, what is the length of the brace you need to cut? When solving this problem, be sure to show all your work.

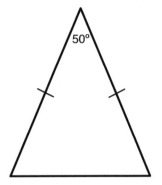

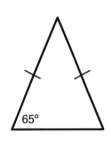

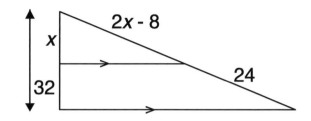

496. △*TUV* and △*WXY* are isosceles triangles. Is △*TUV* similar to △*WXY*?

498. Find the value of *x* in the figure shown above.

497. What happens to the circumference of a circle if the radius is doubled?

499. Draw a net for a regular tetrahedron.

500. A certain right circular cylindrical container holds 24 gallons of water and is 30 inches tall. One gallon of water has a volume of 231 cubic inches. To the nearest inch, what would be the radius of the container described above? (Let $\pi = 3.14$.)

    a. 6 inches
    b. 7 inches
    c. 8 inches
    d. 11 inches

501. The dragonfly is one of the fastest insects in the world. It can fly at speeds of up to 60 miles per hour. How many meters per second is 60 miles per hour?

    a. 16.09 meters per second
    b. 26.82 meters per second
    c. 53.64 meters per second
    d. 96.56 meters per second

502. An Astronomical Unit (AU) is the mean distance between the Earth and the Sun. This distance has been calculated to be 149,597,870.691 kilometers. To the nearest million miles, how many miles is one AU?

    a. 73,000,000 miles
    b. 93,000,000 miles
    c. 99,000,000 miles
    d. 240,000,000 miles

503. A light year is the distance that light can travel in one year. Light moves at a velocity of 300,000 kilometers per second. To the nearest minute, how long will it take light to travel two AUs?

    a. about 8 minutes
    b. about 17 minutes
    c. about 51 minutes
    d. about 310 minutes

504. The amount of garbage recycled in the United States varies directly with the number of people who recycle it. It is estimated that on average 50 people produce 2.5 tons of recyclable garbage annually. Approximately how many tons of recyclable garbage are produced annually by 200,000 people?

    a. 4,00 tons
    b. 10,000 tons
    c. 100,000 tons
    d. 4,000,000 tons

505. Michelle is flying a kite directly over her friend Jenn who is standing 100 meters away. If she holds the kite string down to the ground, it makes an angle of 42° with the ground. How high is Michelle flying the kite?

    a. 67 meters
    b. 74 meters
    c. 90 meters
    d. 111 meters

506. A cheetah's average speed while chasing prey is 72 miles per hour. If a cheetah runs for 3 minutes and captures its prey, how many miles does it run?

    a. 2.5 miles
    b. 3.6 miles
    c. 216 miles
    d. 216 miles

507. A person who weighs 60 kilograms burns 300 calories in 30 minutes of walking and burns 1.5 times as many calories in 30 minutes of jogging. How many calories does a person who weighs 60 kilograms burn in one hour of jogging?

    a. 450 calories
    b. 600 calories
    c. 750 calories
    d. 900 calories

508. Six-foot-tall Matt casts a 54-inch shadow. How tall is his friend if his shadow is 6 inches longer than Matt's? (Assume the shadows were measured at the same time of day.)

    a. 5 feet, 2 inches
    b. 6 feet, 2 inches
    c. 6 feet, 6 inches
    d. 6 feet, 8 inches

509. An investment of $2,400.00 earns $168.00 in interest in two years. What is the interest rate on the investment?

    a. 3.5%
    b. 7%
    c. 14%
    d. 35%

The troy system of weights is used for precious metals and gemstones. The troy pound is divided into twelve ounces, and each ounce contains 480 grains.

510. How many grains are in one troy pound?

    a. 4,660
    b. 5,760
    c. 6,960
    d. 7,680

511. The avoirdupois weight system is based on the 16-ounce pound and contains 7,000 troy grains. Based on this information, how many avoirdupois pounds are in one troy pound?

    a. .5250
    b. .7500
    c. .8229
    d. 1.2153

512. If one troy ounce of gold costs $569.40, how much would one avoirdupois ounce of gold cost?

    a. $427.05
    b. $518.98
    c. $691.94
    d. $711.75

Use the table shown below to solve the following problems.

Currency	Foreign Currency in US Dollars	US Dollars in Foreign Currency
Euros	1.2541	.7974
Swiss Francs	.8072	1.2389

While Brooke was on vacation in Germany, she bought two kilograms of German chocolate for eight euros per kilogram. While Brooke was in Switzerland, she bought two kilograms of Swiss chocolate for twelve Swiss francs per kilogram.

513. How much did Brooke pay for the German chocolate in dollars per pound?

   a. $4.55 per lb.
   b. $6.37 per lb.
   c. $12.76 per lb.
   d. $20.07 per lb.

514. How much did Brooke pay for the Swiss chocolate in dollars per pound?

   a. $.80 per lb.
   b. $1.78 per lb.
   c. $4.39 per lb.
   d. $5.44 per lb.

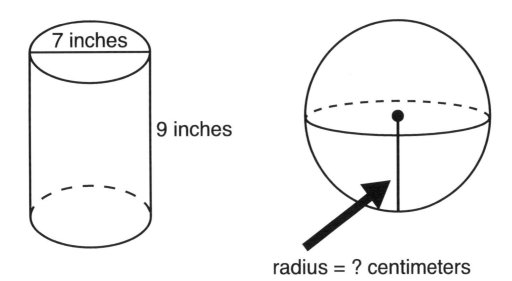

7 inches

9 inches

radius = ? centimeters

515. A right circular cylinder, as shown in the above diagram, has a diameter of seven inches and a height of nine inches. If a certain sphere has the same surface area as this cylinder, what would be the radius of this sphere in centimeters, to the nearest centimeter? (Let $\pi = 3.14$.)

    a. 9 centimeters
    b. 10.5 centimeters
    c. 12 centimeters
    d. 15 centimeters

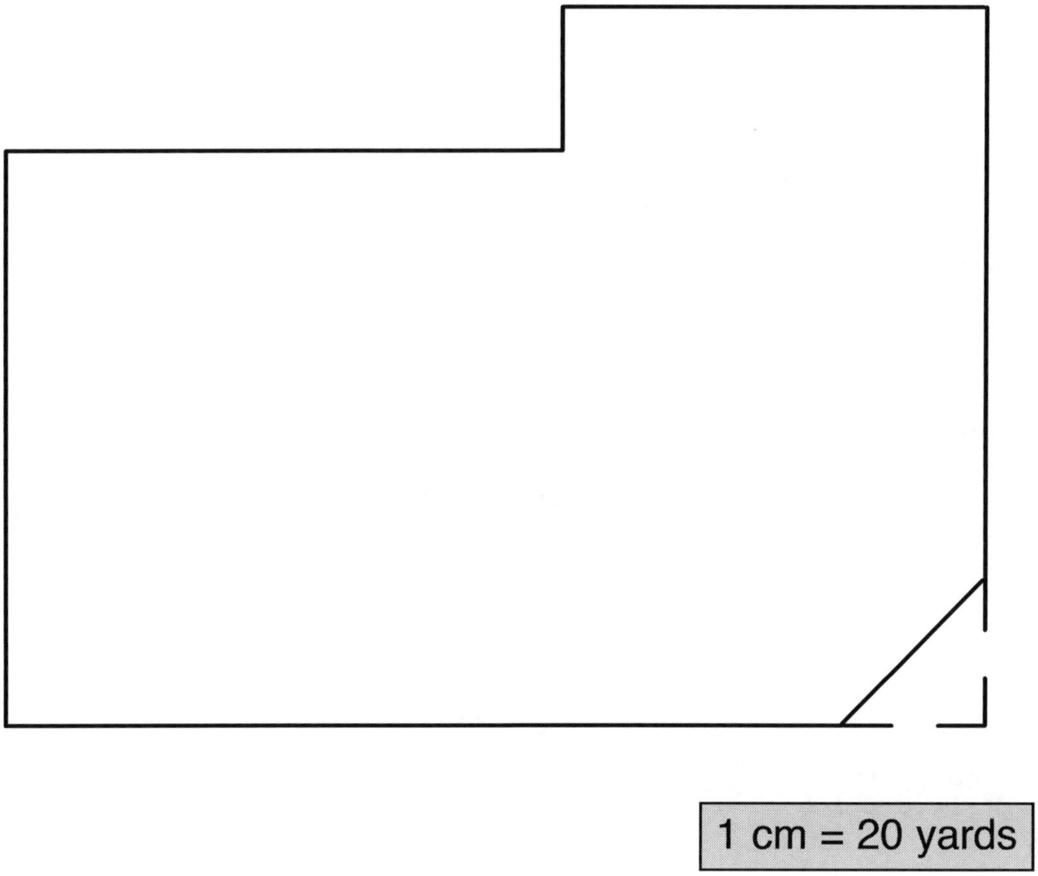

1 cm = 20 yards

516. An area is to be cleared in Milford to build a new park. The area is represented in the scale drawing shown above. Which of the following would be the MOST REASONABLE estimate of the actual area of this park? (Use a centimeter ruler to help solve this problem.)

a. 32,000 square yards
b. 39,000 square yards
c. 44,000 square yards
d. 53,000 square yards

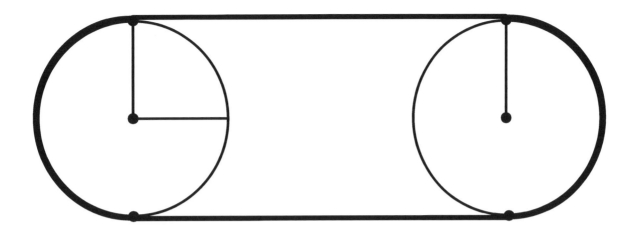

517. A repairperson needs to fix a machine belt that fits around two wheels as shown below. How long, in inches, is the belt he needs? (Use an inch ruler to help solve this problem.)

    a. $2\pi + 8$
    b. $\pi + 8$
    c. $4\pi + 4$
    d. $2\pi + 10$

518. Juan wants to blow up a picture of a painting for a presentation he is making in class. The original size of the picture is 20 inches by 30 inches. Juan wants to quadruple the area of the original picture but keep the same proportions. What will the new dimensions of the picture be?

    a. 80 inches by 120 inches
    b. 40 inches by 60 inches
    c. 48 inches by 50 inches
    d. 120 inches by 20 inches

519. A boat is a distance of 65 meters away from a lighthouse. The angle from the surface of the water to the top of the lighthouse is 37°. What is the height of the lighthouse?

521. Point C cuts the line segment AB into two segments so that the ratio of segment AC to segment CB is five to eight. Find the length of segment CB if the length of segment AB is 26 centimeters.

520. A concrete block is 2 feet wide and 1.5 feet long. To manufacture one block, it requires 0.2 pounds of concrete per cubic foot. If one block weighs eight pounds, calculate the height of the block.

522. How many more minutes will it take to complete a 20-mile drive at an average speed of 50 miles per hour than at an average speed of 60 miles per hour?

Use the table shown below to solve the following problems.

Currency	Foreign Currency in US Dollars	US Dollars in Foreign Currency
Japanese Yen	.008675	115.27
South Korean Won	.001040	961.54

523. Which of the following amounts of foreign currency is worth MORE in US dollars, 2,000,000 Japanese yen or 15,000,000 South Korean won? When solving this problem, be sure to show all your work.

524. ABOUT how many Japanese yen would be needed to match the US-dollar equivalent of 38,750,000 South Korean won?

169

525. A home-and-garden store sells two types of fertilizers in a box. A box of Growth Spurt measures 15 inches by 18 inches by 9 inches and sells for $27.00. A box of Fantastic Flowers is 12 inches by 15 inches by 6 inches and sells for $21.75. Which box is the better deal in terms of price per cubic inch? Show your work or explain how you arrived at your answer.

527. A fish tank is 30 centimeters by 24 centimeters by 70 centimeters. How many liters of water are necessary to fill the fish tank if one liter equals 1,000 cubic centimeters?

526. A 13 meter rope from the top of a flagpole reaches to the end of the flagpole's 5 meter shadow. How tall is a nearby lamppost if it has a shadow of 6.5 meters? (Assume the shadows were measured at the same time of day.)

528. A person 5 feet 3 inches tall casts a 3-foot shadow. At the same time, a tree casts a 9-foot shadow. What is the height of the tree?

529. Below is the floor plan of a new house. You are told that the scale of the drawing is 1 cm = 12.5 feet. You wish to install hardwood floors throughout the house and to get a cost estimate, you need to measure the area of both floors. Find the area of the house in square feet. Round your answer to the nearest square foot. When solving this problem, be sure to show all your work.

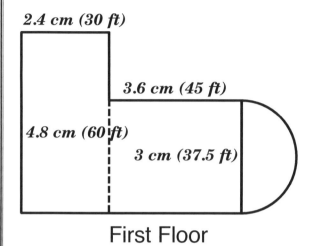

First Floor

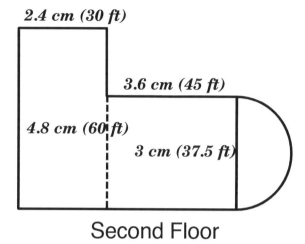

Second Floor

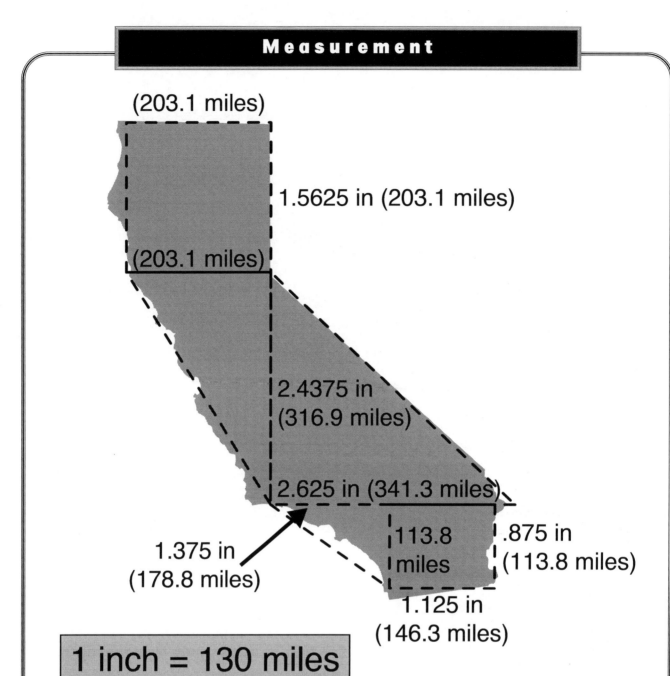

(203.1 miles)

1.5625 in (203.1 miles)

(203.1 miles)

2.4375 in
(316.9 miles)

2.625 in (341.3 miles)

1.375 in
(178.8 miles)

113.8
miles

.875 in
(113.8 miles)

1.125 in
(146.3 miles)

1 inch = 130 miles

530. Approximate the total area of California using the map and scale above. When solving this problem, be sure to show all your work.

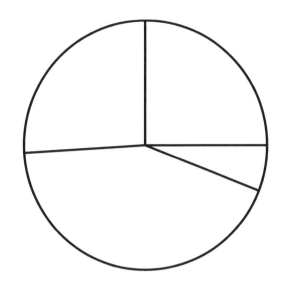

Ice Cream
Vanilla
Chocolate
Strawberry
Coffee
Black Raspberry

Syrup
Chocolate
Vanilla
Mocha

531. The above circle graph most accurately represents which of the following situations?

   a. Michelle spends 20% of her monthly income on utilities, 25% on food, 25% on student loans, and 30% on rent.
   b. The student council is made up of 6% freshmen, 25% sophomores, 27% juniors and 42% seniors.
   c. In the election for freshmen class president, Chris received 22% of the vote, Meredith received 90%, Joe received 98%, and Eddie received 150%.
   d. In a recent survey on favorite sports, 32% of those surveyed chose soccer, 30% chose football, 30% chose baseball and 8% chose hockey.

532. Debbie is going to buy a milkshake. If a milkshake consists of one flavor of ice cream and one flavor of syrup from the above table, how many different kinds of milkshakes are possible?

   a. 8
   b. 12
   c. 15
   d. 16

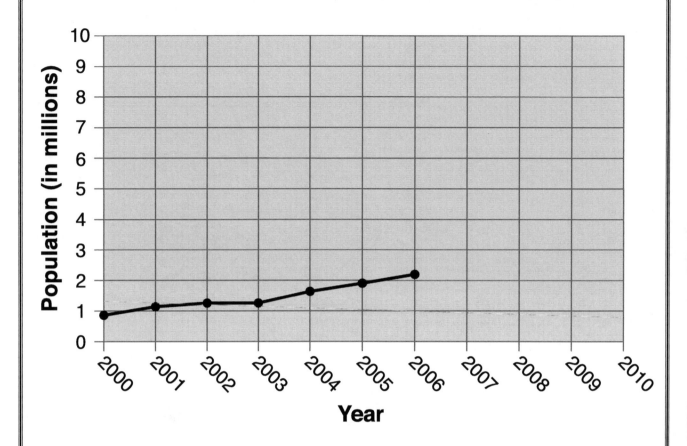

533. The line graph shows the estimated population of a city from 2000 to 2006. If the rate of increase in the population continues, which of the following is the BEST ESTIMATE of the population of the city in 2010?

    a. 2.5 to 3 million
    b. 3 to 3.5 million
    c. 4.5 to 5.5 million
    d. over 7 million

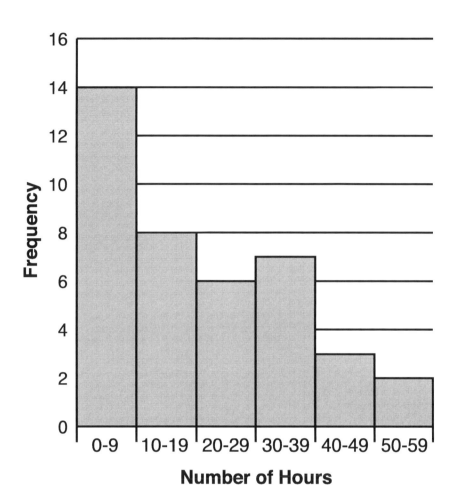

534. Each of the following is shown in the histogram above EXCEPT

    a. The interval 0-9 contains the most students.
    b. Two students work between 50 and 59 hours a week
    c. Twelve students work 30 or more hours a week.
    d. The median of the data is contained in the interval from 20 to 29.

Giovanni and Pedro interviewed 45 students to find out their favorite type of music. Their results are shown in the graph below.

Music	Number of Students
Rock	2
Rap	15
Country	7
Blues	2
Hip Hop	19

535. They want to show this data in a circle graph. What central angle should be used for the section representing hip hop?

a. 19°
b. 76°
c. 120°
d. 152°

536. If there are 2 candidates running for class president and 4 for vice-president, how many different president/vice-president combinations are possible?

a. 6
b. 8
c. 20
d. 12

537. If each number in a data set is increased by 3, which of the following is a true statement?

I. The mean is increased by 3.
II. The mean is unchanged.
III. The range is increased by 3.
IV. The median is increased by 3.

a. I only
b. III only
c. I and III only
d. I and IV only

538. Recent daily low temperatures in Boston are: 53°, 49°, 44°, 53°, 40° and 47°. What is the median of the data?

a. 47°
b. 47.7°
c. 48°
d. 53°

539. A canister contains 10 blue marbles, 6 red marbles, and 8 yellow marbles. If Dorothy draws a marble, puts it back in the canister, and then draws another marble, what is the probability that she draws a red marble both times?

    a. 1/4
    b. 1/8
    c. 1/16
    d. 5/92

541. A spinner has eight equal sections colored green and red. If the spinner lands on green on 16 out of 40 spins, which of the following is most likely the number of green sections on the spinner?

    a. 2
    b. 3
    c. 4
    d. 5

540. A meteorologist is analyzing a data set of the daily amount of rainfall in San Francisco over a given two-week period. Which measurement could the meteorologist use to best show that the daily rainfall remained almost constant?

    a. mean
    b. median
    c. mode
    d. range

542. Mr. Joyce recorded the national average price of gasoline each day for a month. Which measurement did he use to determine that the average price of gasoline varied by $0.34 during the month?

    a. range
    b. mode
    c. median
    d. mean

There are 24 students enrolled in a college class entitled Discrete Mathematics. The line plot shows the ages of the students in the class. Use the line plot to answer the questions below.

```
                                        X
                            X           X           X
                            X           X           X
                            X           X           X
                X           X           X           X
    X           X           X           X           X
    X           X           X           X           X
_____
    17          18          19          20          21
```

543. What is the median of the student's ages?

    a. 18
    b. 19
    c. 20
    d. 20.375

544. What is the probability that a student selected at random to answer a question during a class discussion would be either 18 or 19 years old?

    a. .300
    b. .375
    c. .400
    d. .525

545. A Mexican restaurant offers a "Taco Tuesday" special which includes your choice of one of three tacos: beef, chicken, or vegetable, and your choice of one of two appetizers: nachos or a quesadilla. How many different dinners can be created if each dinner consists of one appetizer and one taco?

a. 3
b. 5
c. 6
d. 9

546. Bashir has test scores of 72, 83, 79, 90, and 81. What must he score on his next test to have an average score of 82?

a. 82
b. 86
c. 87
d. 90

A baseball team's win–loss record from April through mid-August is shown in the table below.

Month	Win–Loss Record
April	16–12
May	15–14
June	17–11
July	12–15
August	9–2

547. Based on the results thus far, what is the probability that the team will win its next game?

a. 1 in 2
b. 18 in 23
c. 23 in 41
d. 23 in 54

Year	Number Applied	Number Admitted
1999	3,824	1,230
2000	3,951	1,270
2001	4,025	1,289
2002	4,078	1,304
2003	4,126	1,315
2004	4,189	1,340

Admission data from a local university is shown above. The university built an additional dorm in 2003.

548. What is the probability that Sally will be accepted if she applied for admission in 2005?

    a. 1 in 3.00
    b. 1 in 3.13
    c. 1 in 3.17
    d. 1 in 3.19

549. In the beginning of 2002, Tad turned 12. His parents put $2,000.00 into a savings account that earned 3.5% interest compounded annually. If his parents deposit $2,000.00 at the beginning of 2003, 2004, 2005, 2006, and 2007, and the account continues to earn 3.5% interest each year, how much will be in the account by the end of 2007?

    a. $11,100.32
    b. $12,420.00
    c. $13,558.84
    d. $14,520.00

Jim is shopping for a computer monitor. The prices at the different stores are below.

$97.00, $95.00, $82.99, $101.50, $92.50, $100.49

550. Which of the following would be the range of prices?

    a. $9.00
    b. $10.00
    c. $17.50
    d. $18.51

551. Which of the following would be the mean amount?

    a. $94.91
    b. $95.73
    c. $96.47
    d. $96.50

552. Which of the following would be the median value?

    a. $94.75
    b. $95.00
    c. $96.00
    d. $96.50

553. Sana reaches into her pocket to get a quarter to make a phone call. In her pocket there are three pennies, six nickels, five dimes, and seven quarters. What is the probability that a coin selected at random is a quarter?

    a. 1 in 3
    b. 1 in 7
    c. 1 in 14
    d. 1 in 21

Dan keeps all of his CDs in his car. Four are rock, three are rap, five are country and one is classical.

555. What is the probability that a CD chosen at random is NOT rap?

    a. 10 out of 13
    b. 10 out of 3
    c. 3 out of 13
    d. 3 out of 10

554. The operator comes on and asks Sana to deposit another quarter to continue her conversation. What is the probability that she picks a quarter the first time she reaches into her pocket?

    a. 1 in 3
    b. 1 in 7
    c. 3 in 7
    d. 3 in 10

556. What is the probability that a CD chosen at random is either country or classical?

    a. 7 out of 13
    b. 6 out of 13
    c. 1 out of 13
    d. 6 out of 7

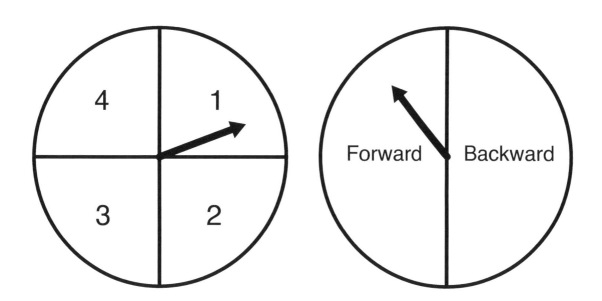

557. Kelli is playing a board game using the two spinners shown above. She spins each spinner once and moves the given number of spaces forward or backward. What is the probability that Kelli will have to move forward more than one space?

    a. 1/2
    b. 1/4
    c. 1/8
    d. 3/8

558. A bag contains 4 red marbles, 5 blue marbles, and 7 green marbles. What is the probability of choosing a red marble?

    a. 1/2
    b. 1/3
    c. 1/4
    d. 1/5

559. A bag contains eight red, six blue, and ten green marbles. Jen reaches into the bag. What is the probability that she will pick a blue marble out of the bag?

    a. 1 in 4
    b. 1 in 6
    c. 1 in 8
    d. 1 in 12

At a local fair, one of the games of chance involves spinning the wheel shown below. Each spin costs $1.00.

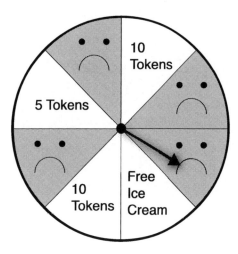

560. What is the probability of winning 10 tokens?

    a. 1 in 4
    b. 1 in 5
    c. 2 in 5
    d. 3 in 10

561. What is the probability of winning no tokens or prizes?

    a. 1 in 2
    b. 1 in 5
    c. 2 in 5
    d. 3 in 10

562. If you spin the wheel 20 times, how many times do you expect to win?

    a. 2
    b. 4
    c. 8
    d. 10

563. A bag contains three tennis balls, five baseballs, and seven footballs. What is the probability that a ball selected at random will be a baseball?

    a. 1 in 3
    b. 1 in 5
    c. 1 in 7
    d. 1 in 10

564. Penny and twelve classmates each put his or her lunch in a brown paper bag. If the bags are all on the table and Penny picks a bag at random, what is the probability that the bag she picks will have her lunch in it?

    a. 1 in 2
    b. 1 in 10
    c. 1 in 12
    d. 1 in 13

1	4	3	4	5	6
2	3	1	6	4	3
6	4	4	3	2	4
1	3	4	6	1	1
1	4	6	6	3	6

Kendrick throws darts at the board shown above. Each throw costs $1.00.

565. If Kendrick gets a prize for landing on a prime number, what is the probability that he will win a prize on a throw?

   a. 1 in 2
   b. 1 in 15
   c. 3 in 10
   d. 17 in 30

566. After one throw, Kendrick can pay $1.00 to throw another dart. If the sum of his two throws is five or less, he wins a bigger prize. If Kendrick's first throw landed on a 2, what is the probability that the sum of his two throws will be five or less?

Made in the USA
Lexington, KY
01 April 2019